Intrapersonal Communication

Intrapersonal Communication

Carolyn M. Del Polito

West Chester State College

Cummings Publishing Company
Menlo Park, California • Reading, Massachusetts
London • Amsterdam • Don Mills, Ontario • Sydney

Acknowledgments

The material covered by note 34 on page 64 is from *Encounters with the Self* by Don E. Hamachek. Copyright © 1971 by Holt, Rinehart and Winston, Inc. Adapted by permission of Holt, Rinehart and Winston.

Cummings Publishing Company, Inc.
2727 Sand Hill Road
Menlo Park, California 94025

Preface

Intrapersonal Communication is the result of eight years of research, teaching, workshops, learning, and living. Through the help of colleagues, friends, and students who have become colleagues and friends, I have come to realize the inevitable impact that a person's self-concept has on the communication process, and thus, on all communication transactions. A communication transaction necessarily begins with the self in the intrapersonal communication process, the focus of this book. Since the self-concept and the intrapersonal process are basic to all communication situations, this book can be integrated into any course concerned with oral communication (fundamentals, public communication, small group communication, etc.) or written communication (fundamentals, creative writing, journalism, etc.). Indeed, all persons should thoroughly understand the intrapersonal communication process and the role of self-concept in that process.

Objectives are stated at the beginning of each lesson, and the successful achievement of these objectives can mean more than the eventual completion of a course and/or the book; it should help students understand themselves better as communicators and make them more sensitive to the communication of others, thus improving their communication skills.

Lesson 1 examines the **process of intrapersonal communication** and provides a model that clarifies the role of self-concept in the process.

Lesson 2 concentrates on the **development of self-concept.**

Lesson 3 underscores the importance of **self and other perception.**

Lesson 4 links **self-understanding and self-acceptance** as integral components for total and effective communication.

Lesson 5 presents six **guidelines for enhancing self-concept**, with the understanding that a person with an enhanced self-concept should be able to communicate more effectively with both the self and others.

My sincere appreciation extends to my colleagues, friends, and students—in classes and workshops—who have given of themselves, providing feedback regarding both the content and exercises included in this book; to the series editors, Bill Brooks and Bob Vogel, for their encouragement and very helpful suggestions; and to Gene, my husband, for his patience and understanding under combat, book-writing conditions.

C.M.DP.

To the Student

We hope that reading this book and working the exercises will be a stimulating and challenging experience for you. Objectives are listed at the beginning of each lesson, and exercises carefully designed to help you achieve these objectives are interspersed throughout the text. You will benefit most from doing the exercises conscientiously as you come to them. A programmed review appears at the end of the book. Completing it according to the instructions will do more than act as a review; it will help you to retain the ideas we've presented.

We have found that students using this type of book, where exercises are presented immediately after the theory, score higher in achievement than students using traditional textbooks. If you follow our suggestions, you should improve your ability to communicate effectively as well as increase your knowledge of the communication process.

We wish you success and would like to hear your reactions to the book and your suggestions for future editions.

William D. Brooks
Robert A. Vogel

Editors

Contents

Lesson 1   The Process   1

Intrapersonal Communication: A Model   2
Self-Concept Core   7
Rationale for Learning More about Ourselves   16
Summary   27
Suggestions for Further Reading   27

Lesson 2   The Development of Self   29

Labeling   30
Social comparison   32
Interpersonal Relationships   33
Significant Others   36
Self-Fulfilling Prophecy   36
Criteria for Significant Persons   40
Summary   49
Suggestions for Further Reading   49

Lesson 3   Perception of Self and Others   51

Others' Perceptions of Us   52
Many Selves   60
Reasons for Role-Taking   62
Defense Mechanisms   65
Summary   70
Suggestions for Further Reading   70

Lesson 4   **Self-Understanding**   **71**

Self-Acceptance   74
Social Sensitivity   77
Active Listening   77
Honest Communication   80
Self-Disclosure   81
Summary   93
Suggestions for Further Reading   93

Lesson 5   **Self-Enhancement**   **95**

Six Guidelines for an Enhanced Self-Concept   97
Conclusion   113
Summary   115
Suggestions for Further Reading   115

Programmed Review   **116**

Lesson 1   116
Lesson 2   117
Lesson 3   118
Lesson 4   120
Lesson 5   121

Notes   **122**

Index   **127**

Lesson 1

The Process

Objectives

Upon completion of this lesson, you should be able to:

1. Define intrapersonal communication.

2. Explain the process of intrapersonal communication.

3. Define self-concept.

4. Explain the role of self-concept in the intrapersonal communication process.

5. Explain the rationale for understanding and learning more about your "self."

6. Explain more fully "who you are."

1

I can't believe it. Back in school again after six years in radio.
U.S. history at 8 in the morning. Oops. He said "Jim." That's
me. "Present." How can the instructor go so fast this early in the
morning? I didn't even have time for a cup of coffee. Everyone
here looks so self-confident. Look at that guy in the black turtle-
neck with his feet on the desk. You'd think he owned the place.
And that girl with the flaming hair. I feel like a wrinkled old pud-
ding. Oh God. They're all taking notes. Notes. I've barely put
pen to paper in the last six years. Guess I'd better put some of this
down, but I don't even know what to write. Looks like everybody
else has a knack for this, and I don't even know what's important.
Why did I quit my job? I must be crazy to give up martini lunches,
free evenings, and a good paycheck for this. Do I really belong
here?

This example illustrates communication in its most basic and perhaps
its purest form—communication with oneself, or *intrapersonal communica-*
tion. Before we can comprehend the complexities of communication with
others (whether it be with one other person, with a small group of individuals,
or with a large audience in a public speaking or mass communication situation), we must first understand how we communicate with ourselves. In
Applbaum's words, "communication patterns in ourselves are the basis for
our processes of communication with others."[1] (All notes appear at the end
of the book.)

Intrapersonal communication identifies the importance of the individual within the communication process. If we are unaware of how we personally process information and communicate with ourselves, how we attach
meaning to our enivronments and to the communication of others, then we
will surely be unable to understand the more complex process of communication with others. Therefore, to provide a solid framework for studying communication in all situations, this book will describe the intrapersonal communication process, and, more specifically, how you personally communicate
with yourself and how you might improve your intrapersonal communication, thus enhancing your communication with others.

INTRAPERSONAL COMMUNICATION: A MODEL

As stated in the preceding paragraph intrapersonal communication focuses on
the individual within the communication process. In our communication
with ourselves, we process incoming information (in the form of external
stimuli—whether visual, aural, tactile, olfactory, or gustatory; or in the form
of internal stimuli—whether physical or psychological) by selecting, interpreting, and evaluating it in terms of previously acquired information. We
then make decisions about processing further information.

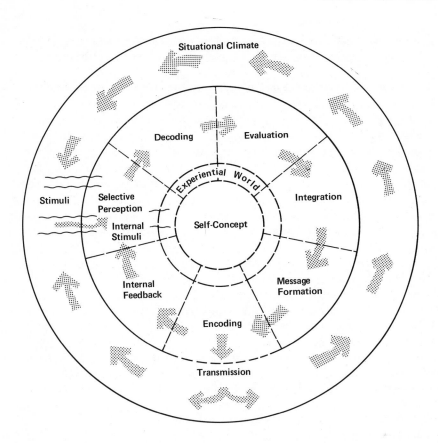

Figure 1.1. The intrapersonal communication process.

Figure 1.1 illustrates the intrapersonal communication process. An individual's self-concept is at the heart of the process, since one's self-concept determines the stimuli selected and the way in which the stimuli will be decoded, evaluated, and integrated into the individual's self-system. The self-concept also determines the message to be transmitted and how it will be sent. As the dotted lines indicate, the self-concept affects and is affected by one's experiential world—all the information accumulated during one's lifetime, including cultural experiences, knowledge, abilities, beliefs, attitudes, and feelings, as well as needs, goals, and expectations for the future. In turn, the person's experiential world affects the entire process of intrapersonal communication. As Figure 1.1 indicates the process is ongoing, circular, and operates as long as stimuli from the situational climate (time, place, and circumstances) or experiential world bombard the individual.

To further clarify the process, let's return to the example at the beginning of the lesson and follow it through the intrapersonal communication process.

As Jim sits in his second college class (situational climate), hundreds of stimuli, both external and internal, bombard his senses: thirty-five people sit facing the professor, who is lecturing and writing an outline on the chalkboard; some students have notebooks open and are writing quickly, while others seem lost in their own thoughts; a train rumbles along behind the building; Jim is hungry and wishes he hadn't missed breakfast. While many of the stimuli may be part of Jim's consciousness, the intrapersonal process does not begin until he *selects* one or more of the stimuli.

Observing the other students in class (external stimuli), he selectively perceives those who are writing in notebooks. He ignores all other stimuli, including the professor's lecture, the girl who is rummaging through her purse, the guy who is staring out of the window, the train, as well as other obviously uncomfortable students.

After he has selected the stimuli, he *decodes* them; that is, he interprets the "codes" or symbols of verbal and nonverbal stimuli to make them meaningful. The effectiveness of Jim's decoding process is determined by his prior experiences (experiential world) with the codes. Since Jim's experiential world is ultimately determined by his perception of self, his self-concept also determines how he decodes or interprets incoming information.

Although the stimuli selected (students writing in notebooks) may be decoded in several ways (e.g., writing letters to friends or doodling), Jim interprets the stimuli to mean that all those students are taking meticulous notes and know exactly what they're doing. Since Jim's self-concept affects his decoding process, and his perception of himself as a student is low, he perceives that he is incapable of performing to the high standards (interpretation) of his peers.

After Jim decodes the stimuli, he *evaluates* them according to their importance to his self-system. He then *integrates* (combines) the stimuli into his existing experiential world. Finally, he acts upon highly important or relevant stimuli in the next stage, the message formation stage. Thus, in our example, Jim evaluates his interpretation of the stimuli (others writing in notebooks) as extremely important to his understanding of the situational climate (college class), and to his perception of himself as a student. Upon integrating the stimuli into his self-system, he *forms a message*.

In the message formation stage he decides on the content of the message; that is, what message will be sent to the self or another. In the next stage, he *encodes* (converts) the message to meaningful symbols, dictating how the message will be sent—the language and code(s) used (verbal or nonverbal), and the medium through which the message will be transmitted (written, oral, mass media, etc.). It is also at this encoding stage that he decides whether to transmit the message to someone else or to allow it to continue in the intrapersonal process for communication with the self only. If the message remains within the self-system, it progresses to the selective perception stage as *internal feedback*. If the message is transmitted outside the self to another person or persons, *external feedback* (from both the self's transmission and the receiver's) will become stimuli for potential selection as the process begins again.

Choosing to allow the message to continue in his self-system, Jim asks himself the question, "Am I where I really belong?" This question (the message) then becomes an internal stimulus for selective perception and the process continues.

Like selective perception and the decoding processes, all subsequent stages of the intrapersonal process are influenced by the individual's self-concept. Evaluation, integration, message formation, and encoding are all influenced by the communicator's perception of self and his or her experiential world (which, again, is influenced by the self-concept).

Exercise 1.1

After last session's exam, Debbie argued with her professor over the fairness of one of the test questions. During today's class, Debbie notices that the professor avoided looking at her, and when they did have eye contact the professor seemed to scowl.

Debbie's exam was returned with a large C— at the top. Debbie gritted her teeth as she quickly left the class, provoked at the seeming unfairness of a professor who could not accept criticism. "That idiot," thought Debbie, "if he would come to class prepared and teach us like he's supposed to, I might have gotten a higher grade! Well, I've had it with incompetent professors. I'm going home and writing to the dean about this injustice."

Analyze the preceding situation, indicating the different stages of intrapersonal communication Debbie is experiencing.

Intrapersonal Stages	Analysis

External stimuli:

Intrapersonal Stages   **Analysis**

Internal stimuli:

Selective perception:

Decoding:

Evaluation:

Integration:

Intrapersonal Stages	Analysis

Message formation:

Encoding:

Internal feedback:

External feedback:

SELF-CONCEPT CORE

We have seen that self-concept is a basic element in the intrapersonal process. But what is self-concept? Self-concept can be defined as the individual's total perceptual appraisal of him or herself (physically, socially, and intellectually). This perceptual appraisal includes all of the ideas, attitudes, and evaluations we have of ourselves. Our self-concept also includes our attitudes toward the roles we assume (whether the roles are important to us or not), as well as our evaluation of ourselves within the individual roles and our satisfaction with those evaluations. Thus, my perception of myself as a college professor is contingent upon the importance I attach to that role, as well as on my satisfaction with my competence as a college professor. Although I may not be conscious of it, my perception (attitudes and evaluation) of myself as a college professor will affect my communication with myself and with others while I'm fulfilling my responsibilities in my job. Similarly, your perception of yourself as a student of communication (a role you assume) consists of your attitudes toward that role and your satisfaction with your own evaluation of yourself as a communication student. Your perception (attitudes and evaluation) of yourself as a communication student will obviously affect your communication with yourself, as well as with your classmates and professor while you are fulfilling that role.

Our self-concept, however, is not based solely on one "self." Rather, as you may have already guessed, there are many different *selves* that make up an individual's *core*, or one's total perception of who he or she is. Self-theorists, Gergen[2] and McCandless,[3] both discuss the many different conceptions of self an individual may possess. As McCandless proposes, the self-concept is "complex, made up of many facets, with each facet differing in importance or reward value, from the others."[4]

Consider your own perceptions of yourself. Do you see yourself the same way in all situational climates? As a student of math? As a student of literature? As an intimate friend? As a son or daughter? As a public speaker? Most definitely, there are differences. You are unique, with a slightly different (perhaps very different) perception of each dimension of your total self. Our individual self-concept is thus composed of all those things we know about ourselves (both consciously and subconsciously), including our *physical, social,* and *intellectual* perceptions of ourselves.

Our *physical perceptions* of ourselves include such things as how we look—fat or skinny, attractive or ugly, or someplace in between; how we move—with a glide or a wiggle, fast or slow, or someplace in between; how we smell—like our favorite soap after a shower, or like hot oil after baking in the sun for the afternoon; how we sound—high or low pitch, breathy or guttural; and how we use our body for physical activities—playing sports, making things, performing tasks. Our perceptions of our physical selves are also determined to some extent by the clothing and accessories we wear.

Exercise 1.2

Consider your *physical* self and your *outer* self by answering the following questions, using this scale: 1 = Never; 2 = Almost never; 3 = Sometimes; 4 = Almost always; and 5 = Always. You may wish to add comments or reactions in the space provided.

1	2	3	4	5	Physical Self
					1. Do you consider yourself healthy?
					2. Are you satisfied with your physical health?
					3. Do you consider yourself attractive?
					4. Are you satisfied with your height?
					5. Are you satisfied with your weight?
					6. Are you satisfied with your shape?
					7. Do you like to be careful about your appearance?
					8. Do you take care of yourself physically?
					9. Do you consider yourself a good athlete?
					10. Are you satisfied with your dexterity and agility?
					11. Are you satisfied with your general body movements?
					12. Are you satisfied with the sports in which you participate?
					13. Are you satisfied with your singing ability?
					14. Are you satisfied with your vocal quality and pitch?
					15. Are you satisfied with your physical self?

1	2	3	4	5	Outer Self
					1. Do you have certain types of clothes that you prefer to wear?
					2. Do your clothes communicate something about yourself?
					3. Do you usually wear accessories (jewelry, scarves, etc.) with your clothing?
					4. Do you consider accessories necessary to the image you project?
					5. Do you wear cologne or perfume?
					6. Are you pleased with the image you project to others?
					7. Are you satisfied with others' reactions to your appearance?

If there are other physical perceptions you maintain about yourself in your "core," or if you have any comments or reactions to the preceding questions, please list them here, using additional pages if necessary.

Along with our physical perceptions of ourselves, our self-concept core also contains our *social* perceptions of ourselves: how we communicate with others—individually, in small groups, or in a large auditorium filled with peers; how we spend our free time; how we relate to our partners, parents, siblings, friends, and professors; how we handle our emotions.

Exercise 1.3

Examine your *social* perceptions and evaluations by completing the following questions, again using this scale: 1 = Never; 2 = Almost never; 3 = Sometimes; 4 = Almost always; and 5 = Always. You may wish to add additional comments or reactions in the space provided.

1	2	3	4	5	Social Perceptions
					1. Do you consider your family life happy?
					2. Do you have responsibilities to your family?
					3. Is there trust among the members of your family?
					4. Are you an important member of your family?
					5. Are you satisfied with your family relationships, includ your involvement and interest in those relationships?
					6. Do you have values, attitudes, and/or ideals which are similar to those of your family?
					7. Do you consider yourself cheerful and friendly?
					8. Do you consider yourself calm and easygoing?
					9. Do you consider yourself confident?
					10. Do you consider yourself popular with members of the opposite sex?
					11. Do you consider yourself popular with members of the same sex?
					12. Do you usually get along with others?
					13. Are you concerned about other people?
					14. Do you try to understand the other person's point of view?

Exercise 1.3 (Continued)

1	2	3	4	5	Social Perceptions
					15. Do you feel comfortable with others?
					16. Are you satisfied with your relationships with others?
					17. Do you have good friends?
					18. Are you an important person to your friends?
					19. Are there any similarities between you and your friends (attitudes, values, beliefs, etc.)?
					20. Do you enjoy belonging to groups in college?
					21. Do you enjoy belonging to groups out of college?
					22. Are you overly sensitive to others' comments?
					23. Do you express your emotions openly?
					24. Do you forgive others easily?
					25. Are you able to solve your problems without too much difficulty?
					26. Are you satisfied with the ways you handle your emotions?

If there are other social and emotional perceptions you have about yourself, or if you have any comments or reactions to the preceding questions, please list them here, using additional pages if necessary.

The final ingredient in our self-concept core, along with our physical and social perceptions, is our mental or *intellectual* perception of ourselves. This includes how competent we feel with academic and nonacademic materials, how we respond to the attitudes, values, and beliefs of others and ourselves, as well as how we perceive our moral and ethical behaviors. In addition, we develop positive or negative attitudes, liking or disliking these perceptions of ourselves.[5]

Exercise 1.4

Examine your intellectual perceptions and evaluations by completing the following questions, again using this scale: 1 = Never; 2 = Almost never; 3 = Sometimes; 4 = Almost always; and 5 = Always. You may wish to add comments and reactions in the space provided.

1	2	3	4	5	Intellectual Self
					1. Do you consider yourself a logical, rational thinker?
					2. Do you consider yourself open-minded?
					3. Do you consider yourself a competent student?
					4. Are you satisfied with your math and science abilities?
					5. Are you a competent reader?
					6. Are you a talented writer?
					7. Are you a talented speaker?
					8. Are you satisfied with your communication abilities?

Exercise 1.4 (Continued)

1	2	3	4	5	Intellectual Self
					9. Do you consider yourself competent in the fine arts?
					10. Do you consider yourself competent in the liberal arts?
					11. Are you satisfied with your willingness to listen to and to discuss different attitudes, values, and beliefs?
					12. Are you satisfied with your grades?
					13. Are you satisfied with what you're learning in college?
					14. Are you satisfied with what you're learning out of college?
					15. Are you satisfied with others' reactions to your intellectual abilities?
1	2	3	4	5	Moral-Ethical Self
					1. Do you consider yourself honest and trustworthy?
					2. Do you consider yourself religious?
					3. Are you satisfied with your moral and ethical behavior?

If there are other intellectual and moral perceptions you have about yourself, or if you have any comments or reactions to the preceding questions, please list them here, using additional pages if necessary.

Exercise 1.5

Now that you have had an opportunity to examine your physical, social, and intellectual perceptions of yourself, how might you describe yourself to others? Who are you? List five key dimensions about yourself in the spaces provided. You can use five words, phrases, pictures, or symbols to describe *who you are.*[6] For example, if you perceive yourself as usually happy, you might draw a picture of a smiling face.

Who Am I?

Examine your dimensions that you have just listed. Do any refer to how you perceive yourself *physically*? *Socially* (in your interactions with your friends, your professors, or your co-workers)? *Intellectually*? As you progress through the book, continue to question yourself and, as you discover a new dimension, return and include it here. In this way, you'll be able to fill in all the pieces of your self-concept core, which is the essence of you.

RATIONALE FOR LEARNING MORE ABOUT OURSELVES

Why should we be concerned with learning more about ourselves, with understanding how we perceive ourselves, with learning about our self-concept? Why be concerned with our development as a person? Why not let it "just happen"? The rationale for learning and understanding more about ourselves is predicated on one basic assumption: we need to know, understand, and accept ourselves before we can begin to communicate with ourselves and others effectively.

To *know* ourselves, to discover who and what we are and why we think and act the way we do, we must learn how we are unique, determining the qualities we share in common with our parents, spouses, siblings, and friends and determining the qualities we possess that are different from theirs. In our search for understanding ourselves, we want to maintain some control over our individual destinies. We shall find, however, we can not "go it alone." We need others—other unique persons—to help us discover who we are. We grow, develop, and mature into fully functioning human beings as we *communicate* with others.

We need human contact and interaction. There are numerous examples of people, particularly young children, who, deprived of contact with other human beings, became physically, mentally, and/or emotionally bankrupt; some even died. As communication scholars, Stewart and D'Angelo, point out, ". . . we don't become fully human all by ourselves; our humanity develops in relationship with others."[7]

The way we behave and communicate with ourselves and others is *directly* influenced by our perceptions of ourselves.[8] We communicate our different selves to others. We communicate who we are (our perceptions, attitudes, values, and beliefs) much more often than we communicate content information, whether we're on the tennis courts, in our rooms studying for an exam, or talking with a close friend on the telephone. Often, we communicate this inner information through our nonverbal behavior, such as facial expressions, eye expressions, gestures, posture, spatial distances, etc. Because we communicate our different selves to others, we should gain as much information about ourselves as we can to fully understand what we are transmitting to others.

Self-concept is an inseparable link in our communication with ourselves and others for another reason: our perceptions of our different selves develop primarily through our interactions, our communication, with others.[9] We obtain feedback regarding others' perceptions of us, and this is stored in our experiential banks for future reference. At the same time, we're also gaining new insights into others, learning about their unique qualities. By understanding ourselves and others, we will begin to realize that not everyone else thinks, feels, and reacts as we do.

Although our self-concept becomes quite stable over time, it can be modified.[10] We have the potential to change negative or unrealistic attitudes about ourselves and replace them with more positive, healthier attitudes. As we learn more about ourselves, understand ourselves, and accept who we are, we increase our effectiveness in communicating with ourselves and with others.

Self-concept, the directing force in our communication with ourselves as well as with others, is also the directing force for all our behaviors and, therefore, the core of intrapersonal communication. It seems natural and imperative, then, that our primary attention be directed to understanding ourselves if we are to understand our communication with ourself and others. However, the self "can only be understood in terms of relationships with others."[11] Noted communication writers, Brooks and Emmert, describe this ongoing, circular process:

> We tend to be what we think we are; we think we are whatever we say to ourselves; and much of what we say to ourselves is what we hear and see others saying about us or to us.[12]

Therefore, although our topic is intrapersonal communication, we will undoubtedly need to discuss our relationships with others to fully understand our relationship with ourselves.

This book, then, will examine self-concept theory, focusing on the development of self-concept in Lesson 2. How self-concept affects our selective perception (without which the intrapersonal process cannot begin) is discussed in Lesson 3, and how we can better understand ourselves and thus better understand our communication with ourselves as well as with others is examined in Lesson 4. Finally, how we can improve our self-concept and thus improve our intrapersonal and interpersonal communication is the focus of Lesson 5.

Developing into the persons we want to become is a life-long process. We are all constantly changing and growing, and our perceptions of ourselves are constantly changing, even if only in a minute way. *Intrapersonal Communication* should, however, help you to understand the intricate process of intrapersonal communication and also demonstrate how you can grow, develop, and mature into the person you want to become.

Exercise 1.6

This exercise will indicate how you perceive yourself as a communicator. It will also determine how satisfied you are with that perception, as well as how important the issue expressed in the statement is to you. Mark your responses to each item on Answer Sheet A, which follows the questionnaire. Answer Sheet B should be used when you've completed the book, to determine if any changes occurred in your perception of yourself as a communicator.

Read each statement in the questionnaire carefully and then select one of the seven alternatives for each dimension (perception, satisfaction, and importance) listed after the statement. Move rapidly from one item to the next and give your initial reaction to each item. If you have never experienced the situation in the statement, indicate how you *think* you would feel in that situation. Do not be concerned with a "correct" answer—there are none.

The following directions define the seven alternatives and demonstrate how to use the answer sheet.

Sample Item: I think I express my ideas clearly.

Almost never	____ 1	____ 2	____ 3	____ 4	____ 5	____ 6	____ 7	Almost always
Extremely unsatisfied	____ 1	____ 2	____ 3	____ 4	____ 5	____ 6	____ 7	Extremely satisfied
Extremely unimportant	____ 1	____ 2	____ 3	____ 4	____ 5	____ 6	____ 7	Extremely important

If you believe you *almost always* express your ideas clearly, mark 7 on your answer sheet in Column 1 under "Perception Scale." If you believe you *almost never* express your ideas clearly, mark 1 in Column 1 on your answer sheet. If you believe you express your ideas clearly half the time, then mark 4 in Column 1. Mark 2 or 3 if you believe your response should be somewhere between "almost never" and the center point (4). Mark 5 or 6 if you believe your response should be somewhere between the center point and "almost always."

Similarly, with the "Satisfaction Scale" indicate where you perceive yourself along the continuum, marking your response in Column 3 of your answer sheet. (Note that you are to skip Column 2 at this time.) Indicate how satisfied, from *extremely satisfied* to *extremely unsatisfied*, you are with how clearly you express your ideas.

On the "Importance Scale," indicate how important, from *extremely unimportant* to *extremely important*, the issue in the statement is to *you* personally, marking your response in Column 4 of the answer sheet. Do not be concerned with what others might consider important. Again, our goal is for *your* personal improvement, and to reach that goal we need to learn your honest perceptions of yourself and the importance of those perceptions.

Scoring: Do not worry about determining your score until you have completed the entire questionnaire. Scoring is used only to help you compare your individual item scores on Answer Sheet A with your completed Answer Sheet B when you have completed the book. Once again, this questionnaire is strictly for your information, to help you understand yourself as a communicator and learn more about your intrapersonal core.

Inventory of Self-Perceptions as a Communicator

Use Answer Sheet A for your responses. Answers to *how you perceive yourself* should be marked in Column 2; answers to *how satisfied* you are with your perception should be marked in Column 3; answers to *how important* the issue is should be marked in Column 4. Disregard Column 2 until you have completed the entire questionnaire. For each item on the questionnaire,* use the following scale:

Almost never	1	2	3	4	5	6	7	Almost always
Extremely unsatisfied	1	2	3	4	5	6	7	Extremely satisfied
Extremely unimportant	1	2	3	4	5	6	7	Extremely important

1. I find it easy to change my language if I see my ideas are not getting across.

2. I am fearful and tense all the while I am speaking before a group of people.

3. Regardless of whom I am talking to, I am a good conversationalist.

4. I feel pretty confident in my ability to communicate in an informal discussion.

*Adapted from "The Effectiveness of Self-Concept as a Communicator to Effectiveness in Student Teaching," by Sandra Hochel and printed by permission, Purdue Research Foundation, West Lafayette, Indiana.

5. It is hard for me to think of examples which will help clarify whatever I am explaining.

6. I feel I am deliberate in my thought processes.

7. I have trouble forming ideas into words.

8. When other people are talking, my mind wanders.

9. I get up to speak with the feeling that I shall surely fail.

10. My ability to express myself remains pretty much the same regardless of whom I am talking to.

11. I feel inhibited when I am expected to contribute something to a discussion.

12. I think I can effectively use audio-visual aids when speaking before a group.

13. It is difficult for me to tell if the person I am talking to agrees with what I am saying.

14. I express myself in a clear and well-organized manner.

15. I like to share my ideas with others.

16. I find it hard to get people interested in what I have to say.

17. If I feel people disapprove of what I am saying, I find it extremely difficult to express myself clearly.

18. People seem interested in what I have to say.

19. I know when I have expressed my ideas clearly.

20. When listening to a speech, my interest is hard to hold.

21. I know what I want to say but not how to say it.

22. Even if I disagree with a person, I will listen to what he has to say.

23. I have difficulty communicating when in a formal interviewing situation.

24. If people do not understand me in conversation, I am happy to explain.

25. I have difficulty in thinking of an appropriate remark to make in group discussion.

26. I enjoy speaking before a group of people.

27. I have difficulty putting complex ideas into words.

28. When I talk, other people listen carefully.

29. My delivery is hesitant and weak when I speak before a group.

30. When talking with others, I find myself thinking of what I am going to say instead of listening to them.

31. I feel I have something worth saying.

32. I like to observe the reactions of my audience to my speech.

33. I avoid speaking situations.

34. It is easy for me to summarize the main points brought up in a group discussion.

35. Although I talk fluently with friends, I am at a loss for words on the platform.

36. I feel at ease in a group discussion.

37. I believe if I tried hard enough I could effectively communicate with almost anyone.

38. I can listen very well even if others around me are not paying attention.

39. Even if I cannot easily understand what a person is saying, I continue to pay attention.

40. I think I use the best language possible.

41. I find it hard to concentrate for a long period of time on what other people are saying.

42. I fear my hands will shake when I speak.

43. I feel my ideas are important and worth telling to others.

44. I find myself not listening to other people because I am preoccupied with my own ideas.

45. In conversation with another person, I get so wrapped up in trying to understand a particular thing, I lose the train of thought.

Answer Sheet A

Question	Perception Scale 1 Answer	2 Score*	Satisfaction Scale 3 Answer	Importance Scale 4 Answer
1.		+ 0 = _____		
2.		– 8 = _____		
3.		+ 0 = _____		
4.		+ 0 = _____		
5.		– 8 = _____		
6.		+ 0 = _____		
7.		– 8 = _____		
8.		– 8 = _____		
9.		– 8 = _____		
10.		+ 0 = _____		
11.		– 8 = _____		
12.		+ 0 = _____		
13.		– 8 = _____		
14.		+ 0 = _____		
15.		+ 0 = _____		
16.		– 8 = _____		
17.		– 8 = _____		
18.		+ 0 = _____		
19.		+ 0 = _____		
20.		– 8 = _____		
21.		– 8 = _____		

Subtotals:

*To determine your correct "Perception Scale" score, either add zero (+ 0) or subtract eight (– 8) as indicated for each item. Your score for both the "Satisfaction Scale" and the "Importance Scale" remains the same as your response.

Answer Sheet A (Continued)

Question	Perception Scale		Satisfaction Scale	Importance Scale
	1	2	3	4
	Answer	*Score*	*Answer*	*Answer*
22.		+ 0 = _____		
23.		− 8 = _____		
24.		+ 0 = _____		
25.		− 8 = _____		
26.		+ 0 = _____		
27.		− 8 = _____		
28.		+ 0 = _____		
29.		− 8 = _____		
30.		− 8 = _____		
31.		− 8 = _____		
32.		+ 0 = _____		
33.		− 8 = _____		
34.		+ 0 = _____		
35.		− 8 = _____		
36.		+ 0 = _____		
37.		+ 0 = _____		
38.		+ 0 = _____		
39.		+ 0 = _____		
40.		+ 0 = _____		
41.		− 8 = _____		
42.		− 8 = _____		
43.		+ 0 = _____		
44.		− 8 = _____		
45.		− 8 = _____		

Subtotals:

To determine your total score for each scale, add your subtotals and put the total here.

Perception Scale	Satisfaction Scale	Importance Scale

TOTAL SCORES   _____   _____   _____

Remember, your total scores should be used only to compare your initial reactions to the questionnaire with your reactions after you have completed the book.

Answer Sheet B

Question	Perception Scale		Satisfaction Scale	Importance Scale
	1	2	3	4
	Answer	*Score**	*Answer*	*Answer*
1.		+ 0 = _____		
2.		− 8 = _____		
3.		+ 0 = _____		
4.		+ 0 = _____		
5.		− 8 = _____		
6.		+ 0 = _____		
7.		− 8 = _____		
8.		− 8 = _____		
9.		− 8 = _____		
10.		+ 0 = _____		
11.		− 8 = _____		
12.		+ 0 = _____		
13.		− 8 = _____		
14.		+ 0 = _____		
15.		+ 0 = _____		
16.		− 8 = _____		
17.		− 8 = _____		
18.		+ 0 = _____		
19.		+ 0 = _____		
20.		− 8 = _____		
21.		− 8 = _____		
Subtotals:				

*To determine your correct "Perception Scale" score, either add zero (+ 0) or subtract eight (− 8) as indicated for each item. Your score for both the "Satisfaction Scale" and the "Importance Scale" remains the same as your response.

Answer Sheet B (Continued)

Question	Perception Scale 1 Answer	2 Score	Satisfaction Scale 3 Answer	Importance Scale 4 Answer
22.		+ 0 = _____		
23.		− 8 = _____		
24.		+ 0 = _____		
25.		− 8 = _____		
26.		+ 0 = _____		
27.		− 8 = _____		
28.		+ 0 = _____		
29.		− 8 = _____		
30.		− 8 = _____		
31.		− 8 = _____		
32.		+ 0 = _____		
33.		− 8 = _____		
34.		+ 0 = _____		
35.		− 8 = _____		
36.		+ 0 = _____		
37.		+ 0 = _____		
38.		+ 0 = _____		
39.		+ 0 = _____		
40.		+ 0 = _____		
41.		− 8 = _____		
42.		− 8 = _____		
43.		+ 0 = _____		
44.		− 8 = _____		
45.		− 8 = _____		

Subtotals:

SUMMARY

We began this lesson by introducing and defining intrapersonal communication and presenting a model of the process. Self-concept, found to be the
basic element of the process, was defined and discussed as the primary concern of this book. A rationale was presented for learning and understanding
more about ourselves. This rationale was based on the assumption that we
need to know, understand, and accept ourselves before we can begin to
communicate with ourselves and others effectively.

SUGGESTIONS FOR FURTHER READING

Anderson, Camilla. "The Self-Image: A Theory of the Dynamics of Behavior."
    Mental Hygiene 36 (1952): 227-244.

Combs, Arthur W., and Snygg, Donald. *Individual Behavior: A Perceptual
    Approach to Behavior* (New York: Harper and Row, 1959).

Dance, Frank E. X., and Larson, Carl E. *Speech Communication: Concepts
    and Behavior*, Chapter 8, "The Intrapersonal Level" (New York: Holt,
    Rinehart and Winston, 1972).

Gergen, Kenneth J. *The Concept of Self* (New York: Holt, Rinehart and
    Winston, 1971).

Goffman, Erving. *The Presentation of Self in Everyday Life* (Garden City,
    New York: Doubleday and Company, 1959).

Hamachek, Don E. *Encounters with the Self*, Chapter 2, "The Self and
    Perceptual Processes: Theory and Theorists" (New York: Holt, Rine-
    hart and Winston, 1971).

Lesson 2

The Development of Self

Objectives

Upon completion of this lesson, you should be able to:

1. Define the following terms: reflected appraisal, significant others, self-fulfilling prophecy, and selective perception.

2. Describe how an individual's self-concept develops.

3. Describe how your own self-concept developed.

4. List the significant people in your life, explain why they should be considered significant, and analyze their influence on your self-concept.

5. Explain how people maintain cognitive consistency.

Through the exercises in Lesson 1, you had an opportunity to discover more about yourself by examining your present self-perceptions. But how did you develop into the person you are today? How did your self-concept develop? Consider for a moment those influences in your past which caused you to perceive yourself as you do. Do you consider yourself honest? A sharp dresser? Clumsy? A competent but not fantastic athlete? Happy? Why? What determined your attitudes, your perceptions, and your evaluations of yourself?

Exercise 2.1

List at least three reasons *why* you perceive or judge yourself as you do.

1.

2.

3.

The reasons for your self-perceptions probably differ widely. Continue reading and compare your reasons with those discussed in the text. Where do yours fit in?

LABELING

One way we determine our attitudes, our perceptions, and our evaluations of ourselves is through society's *labels* for particular types of behaviors.[13] We learn a great many of society's labels from parents, peers, and teachers, as well as through the media—both the electronic media (radio, television, film) and the print media (newspapers, magazines, books).

Certain behaviors are generally labeled *antisocial*, such as picking a fight at a theater, pouring a drink in the hostess' lap, cheating on an exam, and shoplifting. Other behaviors are labeled *social*, such as stopping at a red light, waiting for a person to finish speaking before leaving the room, and paying for the pack of cigarettes the clerk didn't see you pick up. We further categorize ourselves as fitting into more specific labels, such as gentle, honest, kind, and courteous (social labels) or argumentative, dishonest, and rude (antisocial labels). This categorization is based on our perception and under-standing of society's rules.

Exercise 2.2

Select at least two physical, two social, and two intellectual self-perceptions which are based on a label designated by society. For example, if you cheat on an exam, do you perceive yourself as dishonest because society labels cheating on tests as dishonest?

Physical self-perceptions based on societal labels:

1.

2.

Social self-perceptions based on societal labels:

1.

2.

Intellectual self-perceptions based on societal labels:

1.

2.

SOCIAL COMPARISON

Although labeling supplies us with some of our perceptions, it does not account for all the concepts we have about ourselves. Another way our perceptions of ourselves develop is through what Leon Festinger[14] calls *social comparison*, that is, through our comparisons with others. To help us evaluate our looks, our actions, and our feelings, we examine others' appearances, behaviors, and feelings to determine how we measure up to them. While we probably have sufficient evidence to determine whether we are healthy, we may not be sure whether to consider ourselves "religious," "dull," "idealistic," or "lovable." In these cases, we compare ourselves with others who have been labeled, or whom we consider to have these traits. We continually compare and evaluate ourselves—our worth, our abilities, our personal qualities—with others. It's natural. We need to know how we are special and how we are unique.

Exercise 2.3

Select two physical, two social, and two intellectual self-perceptions that are based primarily on *social comparison*—your comparison of your own abilities, characteristics, etc. with those of others. Include the name of the person with whom you compared yourself. Do you perceive yourself as attractive because you compared yourself with a friend who has been labeled, or whom you consider, attractive? Unattractive?

Self-Perceptions	Based on My Comparison with
Physical	
1.	

Self-Perceptions	Based on My Comparison with
2.	
Social	
1.	
2.	
Intellectual	
1.	
2.	

INTERPERSONAL RELATIONSHIPS

We not only compare ourselves with others, we also seek others' reactions to our behaviors. Thus, an additional way self-concept develops is through our *interpersonal relationships*, i.e., in our verbal and nonverbal communication with others. Through *what* others say and *how* they say it, combined with their gestures and other nonverbal cues, we gain information about ourselves. Thus, our intrapersonal core does not develop on its own; it needs interactions with others.

Like a sponge, we absorb other people's (friends, enemies, professors, parents) reactions to us, and we *imagine* what those people think of us. We also imagine how they judge our particular behaviors, such as our writing for the college paper, dancing the latest steps, or playing in a basketball game. We perceive who we are through the *reflected appraisal* of others. We use other people as a mirror that reflects back reactions to our behavior. For example, after telling a joke to a friend, we may look for a physical response: a broad smile, a laugh. We use our friend as a mirror to confirm the humor of the joke, perhaps also to confirm that we are funny; we can tell a good joke.

Although we usually do it unconsciously, we continually seek others' reactions to our actions, opinions, and beliefs. Recall our intrapersonal model; we selectively perceive others' reactions, decode, evaluate, and integrate their reactions into our existing experiential world and self-concept, and then make decisions about sending subsequent messages. Reactions that we consider relevant or important to the self (even unconsciously) will ultimately affect our self-concept. Thus, we begin to accumulate data about ourselves into what sociologist Charles H. Cooley calls the "looking-glass self."[15] We learn to understand ourselves—who and what we are—through the reflections of other people as we interact with them.

Exercise 2.4

Select three physical, three social, and three intellectual self-perceptions that are based on your interactions with (perhaps reactions from) other people. List the names of the individuals who influenced the particular perception. Be as specific as possible. (Do you consider yourself an excellent musician because your music instructor continually praises you?)

Self-Perceptions	Person(s) Responsible for the Perception
Physical	
1.	
2.	

Self-Perceptions	Person(s) Responsible for the Perception
3.	
Social	
1.	
2.	
3.	
Intellectual	
1.	
2.	
3.	

SIGNIFICANT OTHERS

In the preceding exercise, you were asked to indicate those perceptions of yourself that you felt were based on your interactions (your communication) with other people. Is there anything special about the people who influenced your self-perceptions? According to many self-theorists,[16] our more important relationships are those involving "significant others." *Significant others* are those persons who are important in our lives—those persons whom we care about and on whom we depend to gain information about ourselves. Their expressions of approval or disapproval represent rewards and punishments which reinforce our self-ratings.

Since our self-concept core begins to develop at birth, we should examine its evolution, beginning with our initial interactions. When we were young children, the significant people in our lives were primarily our parents. Our older brothers and sisters may also have played a significant role. According to George Mead:[17] as children, we observe the behavior of significant persons—mother, father, brothers, and sisters—and imitate their actions in our play. We role-played their behaviors as a "mommy," a "rock star," or an "airline pilot," and we either were or were not rewarded. Those behaviors that were rewarded or *reinforced* by our parents and siblings were the ones most likely to be retained. We adopted their behaviors and attitudes as our own.

Our self-concept continued to evolve and develop when we began to attend school. Teachers became extremely influential in helping to define who we were and, therefore, became significant persons for most of us.[18] We looked to our teachers, again usually unconsciously, for rewards and punishments. Today we still desire verbal feedback, either orally or in written comments on assignments, as well as nonverbal reactions—smiles, reassuring nods, pats on the arm—to let us know how teachers perceive us and, therefore, how we should perceive ourselves. Research supports these assertions. Two separate studies, one conducted by Brookover, Thomas, and Paterson,[19] and another by Davidson and Lang,[20] found significant and positive relationships between the students' self-concepts and the perceived evaluations of their teachers. Similarly, Videbeck[21] found college speech students rating themselves as they perceived their instructors would rate them.

SELF-FULFILLING PROPHECY

Teachers are extremely significant for some of us and less important for others. Our peers become more influential as we rely on them for judgments of our behaviors. The class clowns pay little attention to the repeated demands of the teacher, enjoying the laughs and applause of their classmates who reinforce them for their clownish behavior. They fulfill others' expectations, performing as their peers anticipate. Perceiving one's self as needing to fulfill other's expectations (unconscious though it may be) is known as the *self-fulfilling prophecy.*

The cycle of the self-fulfilling prophecy is illustrated by John W. Kinch in his formalized theory of self-concept. He suggests that "the actual response of others to the individual will be important in determining how the individual will perceive himself; this perception will influence his self-conception which in turn will guide his behavior. . . . The behavior that the individual manifests influences the actual response of others toward that individual."* The cycle can be represented as shown in Figure 2.1. Unless this cycle is somehow broken (either people's responses to the class clown's behavior change or the person changes his or her behavior), the person may continue to perceive himself or herself as a clown and the "life of the party," and behave as such for many more years. The person may enjoy this label, but there are other perceptions of the same behavior that may have a negative effect on self-concept, such as troublemaker, clumsy, drunk, etc.

Thus Kinch presents another view of our intrapersonal responses, compatible with our original model. Note that the actual responses of others become the stimuli which are selectively perceived and which may become part of one's experiential world; this, in turn, influences one's self-concept. Since self-concept affects our behavior, and since the message-formation-and-encoding stages of the intrapersonal process are integral parts of all behaviors, the two models are indeed compatible, showing the influence of significant others.

Think about yourself. Who are the significant persons in your life? Are your parents still significant in that they exert a certain amount of pressure in their concern for you? Or have your friends become your primary source

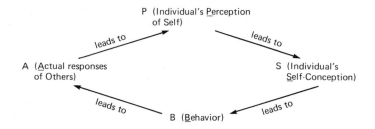

Figure 2.1. Kinch's Model (adapted from John W. Kinch, "A Formalized Theory of the Self-Concept," *Amer. J. Sociology* **68** (1963): 482-483. Copyright © 1963 by the University of Chicago. All rights reserved).

---

*From John W. Kinch, "A Formalized Theory of the Self-Concept," *Amer. J. of Sociology* **68**(1963):482-483. Copyright © 1963 by The University of Chicago. All rights reserved.

of reward and punishment? Perhaps some of your professors are truly significant persons in helping you determine your future goals and expectations.

Exercise 2.5

Reexamine Exercise 2.4. Who are the significant persons for the self-
perceptions you've listed? Use one star (*) for those perceptions where your
parents were influential, two stars (**) for influential teachers, and three
stars (***) for friends who were significant in helping you determine your
perceptions of yourself. What people appear to be most influential in your
life right now? Continue to add to this list as you discover more perceptions
of yourself.

You may want to stop now and consider the degree of influence these
people have had on your life. Do you have certain positive or negative feelings about yourself because of a significant person's reaction to or evaluation
of you? Do you think the evaluations were correct? Do you think you would
act differently, perhaps perceive yourself differently, if that significant person's reactions were different? (Consider again Kinch's theory.)

During discussions about their perceptions of themselves and the causes
for those perceptions, some students have discovered startling facts about
themselves. For many students, elementary-school teachers have had a tre-
mendous impact on how they perceive themselves today. For some, the
effects may last indefinitely. The lasting influences indicate the impact significant people, in this case teachers, have on us.

One of my students perceived himself as a poor writer. When analyzing
why he felt this way (using Kinch's theory), he recalled his third-grade
teacher cracking the ruler over his fingers because of his sloppy "penmanship." Because his teacher's reactions were so negative, Dennis didn't want to
write and so made no effort to learn to write. Not having the experience of
writing about his ideas, Dennis believed he wasn't capable of communicating
his ideas in writing—which wasn't at all true. However, this perception remained until college, when he discovered "penmanship" wasn't everything
and his ideas were valid and worth writing about.

Exercise 2.6

Reexamine your perceptions of yourself in Exercise 2.4. Are they accurate
perceptions? Are any of them negative? Consider the sources of those perceptions to determine how and why you evaluate yourself as you do. In the
following space, list those *negative* perceptions from Exercise 2.4 along with
the names of the *significant persons* whom you feel are responsible for them.
Include your view of the *accuracy* of the person's evaluation.

Negative Perception	Significant Person	Accurate		
		Yes	Somewhat	No

If you feel the significant person's evaluation was inaccurate, there is no reason for you to retain that perception about yourself. If, however, you feel the evaluation was accurate, then this particular perception(s) will need to be worked on and reevaluated as we progress through the book.

We have already discussed the significant people in your life, but for whom are *you* a significant person?

Exercise 2.7

List all those persons who look to you for reaction and evaluation of their behaviors, attitudes, and/or beliefs. They are individuals for whom you are a significant person.

What makes you a significant person for these individuals? Why do certain persons have an influence over your perception of yourself while others do not? Likewise, why are you a significant person for some people and not for others?

Exercise 2.8

List the attributes which characterize a significant person in someone else's life. Remember, a significant person provides us with evaluations which influence our perceptions of ourselves.

CRITERIA FOR SIGNIFICANT PERSONS

Since significant persons contribute to our evaluations of ourselves (whether for our behavior, our attitudes, or our beliefs), it is important for them to have expertise or *credibility* for the activity, attitude, or belief evaluated. "When an appraiser appears to have expertise in any given situation, we are more likely to place our trust in his [or her] evaluations."[22] Consider your communication teacher. If you feel your teacher knows a lot about communication, you will probably accept his or her judgment of your communication ability. You may not accept, however, his or her evaluation of your mathematical ability unless you feel your communication teacher also has expertise in mathematics.

An equally important criterion for a significant person is *personalism*.[23] Those persons who communicate (either verbally or nonverbally) their concern about us as individuals will probably have a significant influence on our self-concept. Because they care, they try to understand us and consider all our actions (including our subtle, nonverbal behaviors) in their evaluations of and reactions to us. If, as you walk into the room, you appear disappointed and dejected, your roommates will probably not jokingly exclaim, "Lost the game, huh?" They are more likely to ask, in a concerned and serious tone, "How did the game go?" It is obvious that your roommates care about you and your feelings and do not try to hurt you. They can be considered significant persons because they have *personalism*.

Exercise 2.9

List the significant persons in your life right now and indicate which criteria apply to each of them. Write C for credibility and expertise and P for personalism. You may find that both criteria apply.

Significant Persons	Criteria

Consider again the people for whom you are a significant person (see Exercise 2.7). Do these people perceive you as a credible individual? Which of these individuals comes to you for your evaluation of or reaction to something they've said, done, or worn? Are you concerned about those persons? Are you tactful? Do you make your evaluations based on how they feel or act on a particular day? If so, you are probably a significant person for them. Consider the impact you may be having on their lives. As a significant person, you may well affect how they perceive themselves and how they may behave in the future.

So far we have discussed the two criteria necessary for someone to be considered a significant person in someone else's life: credibility and personalism. What happens, however, when there is a *conflict* between the other person's evaluation of our performance and our own evaluation of that same performance? Do we believe the other person or our own feelings?

It depends. The degree of credibility is very important when there is a conflict. When we receive conflicting information about ourselves, we may feel pressure to change our opinion of ourselves. If you perceive yourself as a good dancer, you are inclined to believe someone who proclaimed you a great dancer (perhaps you've gotten better). On the other hand, if you don't know your right foot from your left (or so you believe), and someone compliments you on your great dancing ability, you're less likely to believe him or her, unless the individual was *truly* a credible source on dancing—perhaps a friend whose dancing talent you admire.[24]

Another fact which would help determine whether you accept another's evaluation of your dancing performance would be the *number of confirmations* you receive from other significant people.[25] The more often you are complimented on your dancing, the stronger your perception of yourself as a great dancer will become. Consider the following cases.

Arnie considers himself an adequate dancer. At the weekly beer bash, he dances with his favorite partner, Joan. After the dance, a friend, Jim, stops him.

Jim: Hey, man, you're really looking good out there!"

Arnie: Oh? Thanks. (I'm not sure if Jim knows that much about dancing; I've never seen him on the dance floor. But I appreciate his comment, anyway.)

Joan: Hey, Jim's right. You really got into the rhythm."
Arnie: (Smiling) Thanks. (Thinking back, maybe practicing with my sister, Debbie, really helped. I did feel good about how I was dancing, and Joan is a terrific dancer; she does know what she's talking about.) Want to try it again?

Joan: Sure, let's go!

Ben, like Arnie, perceives himself to be an adequate dancer, but things haven't been going well for Ben all week. He failed his calculus test, forgot that his English term paper was due, and had an argument with his girlfriend, Doris, when she asked him why he was depressed. Ben decided to go to the party alone, and seeing Ann, one of the students from his home town, asked her to dance. Afterwards, a friend approached him:

Al: Hey Ben, you were really dancing up a storm—you've really got it together.

Ben: Oh? Not really—it was just a good song. (What does Al know? He's never danced in his life.)

Ann: (Smiling) Ben, Al's right. You really dance well!

Ben: Nah. It was just a good song to dance to, that's all. (Ann's just trying to be nice. She's a good dancer and she doesn't want me to feel inferior. I saw everyone smirking as I was dancing. I must've looked like a fool.) See ya' around, Ann.

Ann: Right, Ben.

Selective perception was operating in both of the preceding situations. We all have strong tendencies to select from our environment (the situational climate) information which provides us with feedback confirming our perceptions of ourselves. Recall how all stages of the intrapersonal communication process are affected by our self-concept and experiential world, represented by the model's broken lines (refer back to Figure 1.1). Our selection of incoming stimuli, then, will be congruent with our self-perceptions.

In Arnie's case, he selected the information he wanted to hear. He had practiced the latest dance with his sister, and he was already fairly confident of his dancing ability, so he accepts the compliments from his friends and begins to perceive himself as a better dancer than he was when he started.

Ben, on the other hand, was already down on himself, so he selected what he wanted to hear—just negative information. He selectively perceived Al's comment as irrelevant, Ann's statement as sympathetic, and the onlooker's smiles as smirks. He maintains his image of himself as a poor dancer not because others' reactions were negative, but because he chose only to select the cues which reconfirmed his perception of himself as doing everything wrong.

Selective perception is one of the primary reasons why an individual's self-concept does not change easily. We tend to select only information which keeps our perception of ourselves consistent with how we believe we should be perceived. Each of us tends to preserve the ideas and attitudes we have already formed about ourselves. This reaction is known as *cognitive consistency*. We strive to be ourselves (as we see ourselves) and live according to the attitudes we have toward ourselves.

According to Leon Festinger,[26] to maintain our self-concepts, to preserve the person we perceive ourselves to be and, therefore, preserve cognitive consistency, we generally react to new information in one of three ways:

1. We may ignore incoming conflicting information, because we feel it doesn't have any relevance or relationship to whom we perceive ourselves to be.

2. We may organize, interpret, and perhaps change the information to fit in with our perceptions of ourselves.

3. We may change our concept of ourselves to agree with the new information.

Referring to the two cases of Arnie and Ben, Arnie reacted to the new information by organizing and interpreting the information to fit in with his perception of himself as an adequate dancer, and even changing his perception of himself slightly, seeing himself now as a better dancer than before. Ben, on the contrary, reacted to the new information by ignoring it, because he didn't feel it had relevance to how he perceived himself—poor in everything, including dancing.

Have you received any new information about yourself recently? How did you react? Did you accept all of the new information? Only part of it? Did you reject it? Why?

Exercise 2.10

Keep a record of any new information you receive about yourself for at least three days. This information may come from friends, family, professors, or others. Along with listing the new information, include the person who offered the information and indicate whether you consider the individual a "significant" person (using the criteria of credibility and personalism). In the last column, indicate your reaction to the new information. Did you accept the person's entire reaction, accept only part of the reaction (indicate which part), or ignore the person's evaluation as irrelevant or inappropriate to how you see yourself? Try to determine why you reacted as you did based on the preceding discussion.

(1) New Information Received	(2) Source (Who)	(3) Significant? (Yes/No)	(4) Reaction

Exercise 2.10 (Continued)

(1) New Information Received	(2) Source (Who)	(3) Significant? (Yes/No)	(4) Reaction

Exercise 2.11

Discuss with a significant person in your life the effect he or she has had on you. Did the person realize the impact he or she was having on your life? Now that you've made him or her aware of this influence, will his or her behavior change? Is he or she pleased to be a significant person in your life? Record both your own reaction and the other person's reaction to the conversation.

My reaction:

The other person's reaction:

Exercise 2.12

Now that we've discussed how you developed into the person you are today, write a detailed essay describing who you are and how you came to be that way.

Exercise 2.12 (Continued)

SUMMARY

In Lesson 2, we have examined the development of self-concept in a general way, and, more specifically, how your self-concept emerged. We have found that the three primary determinants of an individual's self-concept are society's labeling, our social comparison with others, and our interactions with significant others. Because significant others are extremely important in the development of our different selves, we have carefully defined and examined the characteristics of significant persons in our lives. While others' reactions influence our self-concept, our self-concept influences our perceptions of events as well as our behavior. Our need to maintain consistency in our core results in our attempt to eliminate conflicting incoming stimuli.

SUGGESTIONS FOR FURTHER READING

Cooley, Charles H. *Human Nature and the Social Order* (New York: Schocken Books, 1964).

Festinger, Leon. "A Theory of Social Comparison Processes." *Human Relations* 7(1954):117-140.

Festinger, Leon. *A Theory of Cognitive Dissonance* (New York: Harper and Row, 1957).

Kinch, John W. "A Formalized Theory of the Self-Concept." *The American Journal of Sociology* 68(1963):481-486.

Levy, Ronald B. "Relationships within the Self," in Joseph A. DeVito's *Communication: Concepts and Processes* (Englewood Cliffs, N. J.: Prentice-Hall, 1976).

Mead, George Herbert. *Mind, Self, and Society* (Chicago: University of Chicago Press, 1934).

Mills, Judson. "Interest in Supporting and Discrepant Information." Robert P. Ableson, Elliot Aronson, William J. McGuire, Theodore M. Newcomb, Milton J. Rosenberg, and Percey H. Tannenbaum, eds., *Theories of Cognitive Consistency: A Sourcebook* (Chicago: Rand McNally, 1968).

Lesson 3

Perception of Self and Others

Objectives

Upon completion of this lesson, you should be able to:

1. Explain those elements included in your perceptions of others and others' perceptions of you.

2. List and explain at least ten dimensions which make a person unique.

3. Define the terms "roles" and "defense mechanisms."

4. Describe the three primary sources that determine the role a person assumes.

5. Describe, analyze, and evaluate at least eight defense mechanisms we often use.

OTHERS' PERCEPTIONS OF US

Lesson 2 described those influences which helped create the person you are today. Your evolving awareness of who you are and how you developed continues to add to your self-concept core. Lesson 1 demonstrated that the way you perceive yourself will help determine how you relate to and interact with other people. Lesson 2 demonstrated the importance of others' perceptions of us: others' reactions influence the continuity of the cycle represented in Kinch's model (Figure 3.1). But how do we perceive others' reactions to us? Do we perceive correctly these stimuli (others' reactions) which initiate the intrapersonal process? How do others perceive us? As we see ourselves? To better understand ourselves and to effectively communicate with ourselves and others, we need to determine others' perceptions of us.

There are several methods of discovering how other people perceive us. Our first approach will focus on how we see other people. Gaining information about our perceptions of others will clarify how others perceive us and why they do. Additionally, since our perceptions of others determine how we communicate with them—that is, how we react to them, which, in turn, will influence their self-concept—our first priority should be to examine our perceptions of others.

Exercise 3.1

To complete this exercise, you need to select a person you know.

Person's Name: _____

1.   Who is this person?

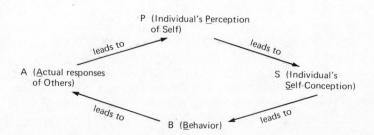

Figure 3.1. Kinch's Model (adapted from John W. Kinch, "A Formalized Theory of the Self-Concept," *Amer. J. of Sociology* **68** (1963): 482-483. Copyright © 1963 by the University of Chicago. All rights reserved).

2.   How do you perceive this person? (List as many characteristics as possible.)

3.   What determines your perceptions of this person? On what information are you basing your reactions and perceptions of this person?

How did you derive your perceptions of your selected person? Through your past experiences with him or her? Undoubtedly, some of your observations were based on what you know about the person from having been with him or her in the past—how he or she behaved in the past, what he or she communicated.

Check your responses to Exercise 3.1. Many of our perceptions are based on what we expect our selected person to be. Also, some of our perceptions are based on who the selected person actually is, as well as on the way the person sees himself or herself.[27]

Others' perceptions of us are also based on a combination of their past experiences with us, what they expect us to be, the way we actually are, and the way we see ourselves. When I communicate with you, I will be communicating with the person I perceive you to be—the person I think you are, and vice versa. You will be communicating with the combination of perceptions you have about me.

John Keltner suggests that "what we actually do when we speak to each other is talk to ourselves."[28] According to Keltner, when I speak to you, what I'm actually doing is talking to my image of you—my perception of who I think you are. (My perception of you *includes* your perception of yourself as I understand it.) It is not until I know more about you that my image of you (stored in my experiential world) comes closer to your image of you. To communicate effectively with you, then, I need to learn how you perceive yourself. Then, instead of communicating with myself alone (or my perception of you), I will be communicating with you (or your perception of yourself). Conversely, for you to communicate effectively with the person you selected for Exercise 3.1, you will need to learn how that person perceives himself or herself.

Exercise 3.2

List some specific things you could do to learn more about your selected person in Exercise 3.1. Would you ask him or her certain questions? Would you watch his or her behavior?

To understand others, we must see their world as they do. That's not always as easy as it sounds. But we must find ways of discovering the dimensions of the other person which make him or her unique. These dimensions can include the person's ideas, attitudes, beliefs, body, voice, and movement characteristics, as well as the person's relationship with others and with himself or herself, the self which is publicly known, and the self which is known only to the person himself or herself.[29]

We can discover another's unique qualities through actual observation of the person's behavior and his or her communication with us and others. We can listen to what the person has to say about himself or herself and others. Listening should also help us collect information regarding the person's ideas, attitudes, and beliefs. We can see what the person does or does not do, how he or she behaves, how he or she interacts with others, what he or she looks like, how he or she moves, etc.

Often we can discover another's unique qualities by listening to the observations of other people. We must be cautious, however, about accepting all incoming information as true. Another's perceptions may not be objective. Remember, each of us perceives the world and the events and people in it differently—we each have a different experiential world. It's wise to discover people for ourselves, or at least accept new information about others as tentative.

As we determine who we are, we evaluate our different selves, or different dimensions of the self, against certain criteria. The criteria include (a) the *actual, observable facts* of the dimension (we see our bodies, we hear our voices, we feel our movements, etc.) and (b) *comparisons* of our different selves or dimensions with the selves or dimensions of others (for example, we compare our ability in track against other track runners). (Lesson 2 describes social comparison as one way in which our self-concept develops.) Thus, we compare our ideas, bodies, voices, movements, and relationships with others with the ideas, voices, etc. of others as one means of evaluating our own selves.

To understand ourselves better, then, we need to gain information about ourselves from other people. Other people's responses give us clues about their perceptions of us. Likewise, to be able to truly communicate with others, we need to obtain information from them regarding themselves. We need to see the world as they do. Also, our communicating our perceptions to them may help them learn more about themselves. Therefore, by observing others, listening to what others have to say about themselves, and opening up ourselves to others, we can gain much information to help us understand ourselves and others, and therefore communicate more effectively.

Exercise 3.3

To discover more information about other people in your communication class, plan and carry out a "Get Acquainted Campaign" by doing the following:

1.   Select someone you don't know very well, someone you haven't had a chance to talk with or listen to. Your partner should agree to get to know you.
     Selected Person: _____

2.   Indicate your present perceptions of your selected partner by completing Chart A, giving as much detail as possible (without assistance from others). Include as many dimensions as you can. (Those facts which make your selected person unique are ideas, attitudes, beliefs, body, voice, movements, relationships, public and private self.)

Chart A

I perceive _____ as a person who:
                    (name of partner)

Likes:

Dislikes:

Cares about:

Believes:

In addition, _____ is (include any
                    (name of partner)
additional perceptions of your partner's unique qualities):

3.   Continue your "Get Acquainted Campaign" and determine a strategy
for obtaining more information about your partner. Your plan should be as
specific as possible, including date, time, place, information needed, etc.
Whatever method you select to gain more information about your partner,

be sure to give yourself enough time for your conversation.

My strategy for getting to know my partner will be:

Some things I want to find out about my partner are:

4.   Before following through with your strategy, complete Chart B for yourself.

Chart B

I perceive myself as a person who:

Likes:

Dislikes:

Chart B (Continued)

Cares about:

Believes:

In addition, I am:

5.   Do you think your partner will perceive you the same way? Explain your response in the following space.

6.   You should be ready now to implement your plan. Remember, your goal is to obtain as much information as possible about your partner. When you have completed your plan, fill out Chart C.

Chart C

Having had an opportunity to talk with and listen to my partner, I perceive
_____ as a person who:
                    (name of partner)

Likes:

Dislikes:

Cares about:

Believes:

In addition, _____ is:
                            (name of partner)

7.   Compare Charts A and C. Have your perceptions changed? Discuss
with your partner those dimensions which remained the same and those

which changed after you got to know each other better. Why are there differences? Explain.

8.   Now, compare your Chart B with your partner's Charts A and C. Did you find more similarities between your partner's Chart C and your Chart B than between your partner's Chart A and your Chart B? Discuss with your partner the similarities and the differences and the reasons for them. Now do the same for your partner's Chart B and your Charts A and C.

Through your discussion and analysis of your charts with your partner, you should have learned not only a great deal about your partner, but also a lot about yourself.

Exercise 3.4

Using the feedback from your partner, indicate any new information you discovered about yourself.

MANY SELVES

From the beginning of Lesson 3, we have discussed how others' perceptions of us are based on their past experiences with us, what they expect us to be, the way we actually are, and the way we see ourselves. The roles we assume in various situations are yet another dimension which influences others' perceptions of us.

Consider for a moment your evaluation of how you perceive yourself as indicated in Chart B. Do your answers and reactions indicate how you feel about yourself all the time? Are these perceptions of yourself the same in different situations: when you're playing your favorite sport, watching TV, taking a test? Probably not. There are undoubtedly certain situations in which some of your responses on Chart B would not hold true. Does that mean you're being hypocritical? Not at all. We each have many different and unique selves, and we change our patterns of behavior to fit particular circumstances.

Those patterns of behavior which are appropriate for specified occasions are classified as "roles." Role-taking is a normal, natural behavior and is necessary in adapting to the many and varied communication situations in which we find ourselves. These roles have developed within our intrapersonal processing systems and are therefore part of our experiential world and self-concept core.

Do you communicate in the same way with your parents, your close friends, your professors? Again, probably not. We all find it necessary to relate specifically to the receiver of our message, to change our mask to fit the person and the situation.

In a routine day, I find myself assuming a variety of roles: wife, teacher, counselor, sister, daughter, friend, cook, shopper, lover. I'm good at some of them. Some I prefer to others. What roles do you assume during the course of a regular day?

Exercise 3.5

List the roles you assume during the course of a regular day.
Day/Date: _____

What determines your roles?

REASONS FOR ROLE-TAKING

There are basically three primary sources which influence our role-taking behavior: the other person, the environment, and our personal motivation.[30] Let's examine each of these influences separately.

The identity of the other person and his or her behavior toward us will determine the image or role we present. We will react to others' expectations of us and to their roles as seen by us. Our parents have certain expectations of the way we should behave when we are reprimanded, while our friends may have entirely different expectations. We tend to behave slightly differently in different roles. We may be walking to class with John, joking and discussing last night, but meeting Terry on the way home, we become intense and philosophical about the state of the economy. We are the same person. However, our past experiences with John and Terry have fostered certain expectations for our behavior, and the presence of these individuals elicits different reactions.

The environment also affects our role-taking behavior. Different settings stimulate different reactions. Consider your own behavior in a religious setting as contrasted to your behavior in a pool hall or a state assembly meeting. Even if the same individuals are present in each of the settings, your roles will still change to accommodate the expected behavior— the expected or usual roles—for each environment.

Our choice of role-taking behavior may be determined also by our specific motives in the relationship. If you were running for treasurer of the student government and wished to be considered trustworthy by your peers, you would act differently than you would if your primary motive were power and superiority. Similarly, if you wished to be perceived as lovable, you would not refuse to hold another person's hand.

Our role-taking behavior, then, is determined primarily by the other person we're communicating with, the environment we're communicating in, and our motives in the relationship. Refer back to Exercise 3.5 in which you listed the roles you assume during a normal day. Are there some roles which you prefer over others? Why do you prefer them?

Exercise 3.6

List the roles you prefer and the reasons for your preference.

Preferred Roles	Reasons for Preference

The roles you've just listed must give you positive, rewarding feelings. Usually, when we assume a particular role, we change our attitudes toward that role based on the rewards we receive for having maintained the role. Also, if we are rewarded for behaving in a particular way, we begin to prefer that mode of behavior, that role. We don't need verbal approval. We may just imagine the positive reactions from others. We may gain reward from our own positive evaluations or from the incentives or motives offered for a particular role. If, while assuming the role of student, we receive high grades, praise from our professors and parents, and admiration and respect from our friends, we will enjoy maintaining the role of student and may consider going on to graduate work. On the other hand, if no one cares about our good grades and we receive little or no verbal or nonverbal reinforcement, we undoubtedly will disregard the student role and select a more rewarding one. We may prefer our role as employee, rather than as student, if we receive more incentive, praise, and financial gain when we work at a local department store.

Besides preferring certain roles, we also tend to identify with the roles. Perhaps you may obtain a supervisory role. That role will require you to act confident, businesslike, and perhaps at times detached from your subordinates. Because you prefer that role (it gives you many different kinds of rewards—power, prestige, financial independence), you identify with the role and may therefore adopt similar behaviors in other situations where your supervisor-like behavior is not strictly required. Imagine the consequences of the supervisor who carries along his or her role to a concert. We need to be flexible in our role-taking and realize that we can identify too strongly with a particular role.

Our desire to be consistent in our perceptions of ourselves may also affect the results of role-taking. (In Lesson 2, we discussed the three different methods we use to maintain our self-concepts.) We strive to remain consistent and live according to the attitudes we have toward ourselves. Therefore, if we are in a situation in which our required role is in opposition to the usual roles we assume, or in opposition to our self-concept, we will probably try to reduce the conflict we feel by changing our ideas about ourselves.[31]

For example, if you perceive yourself as a staunch conservative and then find yourself agreeing more strongly with a professor whose views are liberal regarding revisions of your department's curriculum, you will probably modify your view of your role as a staunch conservative—at least in this particular situation. Or perhaps your role as a member of the college's judicial board requires you to reprimand peers for disobeying dorm regulations. While you originally perceived yourself as having a laissez-faire attitude, now because of your new role and obligations, you perceive yourself as more authoritative, at least when you act for the judicial board. Thus, you reduce your inner conflict and maintain a consistent perception of yourself.

The additional dimension of role-taking, therefore, adds to the complexity of how we are perceived by others. Likewise, the other person's role-taking behavior complicates our perception and understanding of the other person. Yet, in examining all the dimensions we've discussed so far, we can more clearly understand how complex we are and how each of us has not one self-image, but a multitude of dimensions—many selves which can adapt, relate, and communicate in a variety of situations.

Exercise 3.7

List all the roles you've assumed within the last week. Include the kinds of rewards you received for each role, placing one star (*) next to the roles you prefer, two stars (**) next to the roles you identify with, and indicate those roles you have carried into situations where the role was not strictly required. Briefly describe the situation.

Role	Rewards	Role Not Required for This Situation

Another dimension which confuses others' perceptions of us and our perceptions of others is what is known as *defense mechanisms.* These are learned behaviors used to protect and preserve our image of ourselves—to maintain consistency in our core.[32] We dislike finding ourselves in awkward positions; we dislike feeling anxious or threatened in any situation. As self-concept theorist Don Hamachek suggests, defense mechanisms help us maintain our feelings of personal worth by reducing conflict and frustration, particularly when we encounter stressful situations.[33] Thus, part of our core and part of our experiential world are the defense mechanisms we've learned over a period of time. These defense mechanisms, therefore, are instrumental throughout the intrapersonal process, affecting the stimuli we accept, how we decode, evaluate, and integrate the stimuli and determine our further processing of the information.

As we discuss different defense mechanisms,[34] you will notice we all use them at times. They are quite normal and sometimes desirable. We should be careful, however, not to use them excessively; otherwise, they will begin to harm rather than enhance our intra- and interpersonal communication.

How do you defend your self-system? Examine the types of defense mechanisms we incorporate into our behaviors. Are any familiar to you?

Some fairly popular defense mechanisms include projection, rationalization, fantasy, compensation, denial of reality, repression, internalization, and displacement. Let's examine each of these separately.

DEFENSE MECHANISMS

Projection, or "it's not my fault," is blaming someone or something else for our failures or mistakes. Often, we project blame for our inability to learn a new task—whether it be hitting a baseball, typing, or learning a new dance—on our instructor, or on the conditions of the environment, the object we're working with, etc. Bad luck is often blamed for our mishaps.

Students who have not completed their term projects complain there were no books on their topics in the library. A losing team may blame the referee for its disappointing score, while the store clerk, whose register slips do not coincide with the money received, blames the machine. Projecting blame on someone or something else does help us to retain our self-worth. It helps us avoid rejection and feelings of personal failure.

Rationalization, or "there's a reason for it," is similar to projection, but in this technique we invent reasons for not reaching our specified goals. When we rationalize, we also find reasons for doing something we shouldn't. We rationalize for performing poorly on the test by explaining that there was not enough time to finish it; or for not mowing the lawn (it looked as if it were going to rain); or for cutting classes on Friday (the professors weren't going to do anything special anyway). Although rationalizations help us to maintain our self-esteem, we should be careful not to deceive ourselves—a far worse crime than deceiving others.

Fantasy, or "I wish . . . ," is a device used to escape the real world, perceiving the world as we would like it to be, rather than as it actually is. We create Disneyland atmospheres and step into the worlds of our favorite television and movie characters as we watch them solve their problems within the short span of an evening. We should realize, however, that instead of dreaming with our media heros and heroines, we can utilize our fantasy machines much more productively for our own problem-solving and imaginative thinking.

Compensation, or "masking" a "weak or undesirable characteristic by emphasizing a more positive one," is again quite normal.[35] We can hide our inabilities in athletics by focusing our interests on academic areas, and vice versa. The advertising media have provided numerous solutions for our physical, mental, and social weaknesses. There is an answer for everything, from hair which is too dry to the cook who doesn't like to cook. If we're too short for basketball, we may try track; if we're too slow for track, we may try basketball.

Perhaps compensation is one of the more desirable defense mechanisms. By compensating for our weaker characteristics, we can build and strengthen our positive characteristics. If not overused, compensation can help enhance our concepts of ourselves.

Denial of reality, or "hiding our heads in the sand," can be a bit more dangerous if it is used to extremes. Avoiding or refusing to face reality does assist in protecting the self, but it may also keep us from knowing the truth. Turning from the unpleasant sight of an accident and ignoring or disclaiming criticism fit into this category. Sgt. Schultz's lines from the television program, "Hogan's Heroes"—"I know nothing! I see nothing!"— characterizes Schultz's refusal to acknowledge actual occurrences. Other examples include the college student who refuses to admit a hearing loss because of what he or she perceives other persons' reactions will be to his or her wearing a hearing aid; or the woman who refuses to believe she has a heart problem and pushes her physical capabilities to extremes. Hiding our heads in the sand, therefore, may keep us from seeing those things which may help us to live a more fulfilling life.

Repression, or "I can't remember," helps us to be consistent in our self-concept by allowing us to forget those things which are painful or upsetting. A man who has been hurt by a good friend will want to forget all about him and the circumstances leading to their problems. Many times, instead of trying to forget or repress disagreeable circumstances, it is better to confront the problems head on in an attempt to solve them.

Internalization, or "if you can't beat them, join them," allows us to incorporate those characteristics of another individual (or of our social system) that may threaten us. We incorporate as part of our self-system our parents' rules and values: "make sure you call if you can't make your appointment"; "a college education is a necessity for any person in today's world"; "we accept people from all backgrounds in our neighborhood." We incorporate society's rules and values as well: when driving, we stay on the right-hand side of the road and stop at red lights; we also drop our coins into the parking meter. Since we can't beat the system, we join it and internalize the system's rules and values.

Displacement, or "scapegoating," is another defense mechanism in which we shift our reactions and feelings from the intended person or object to a less threatening person or object. When Pat, disgusted with her professor's criticisms, goes home, she growls at her roommate for wearing her blouse. Usually, the two roommates share clothing. However, because Pat feels she can't argue with her authoritarian professor, she takes our her aggressions on her roommate. Rather than displacing feelings on the wrong person, who knows nothing about the situation, it would be more worthwhile to try to solve the problem by discussing our feelings and reactions with the person who originally initiated the problem.

Projection, rationalization, fantasy, compensation, denial of reality, repression, internalization, and displacement are eight common defense mechanisms that can help us to preserve and protect the persons we perceive ourselves to be. In addition, there are three other defense mechanisms which we sometimes use: emotional insulation, reaction formation, and regression. Have you ever used any of these?

Emotional insulation allows us to build strong shields around ourselves so we don't get hurt. Because Chuck was hurt by his girlfriend, he won't allow himself to care or become involved with any other woman. Again, emotional insulation protects us from too many hurts and disappointments, but as we mature, we realize there are risks involved in any close relationship. (We'll talk more about these risks in the next lesson.) Our task now, however, is to make sure our walls are not too high or too thick to prevent meaningful relationships from developing.

Reaction formation, or contradiction, occurs when a person develops behavior patterns and attitudes which contradict his or her actual feelings and attitudes. Reaction formation can be noted in the daughter's comment to her mother that she did not mind going to the store for her when she actually wanted to finish reading the paper; or, when turned down for a date, Andy replies that he was really too tired to go out tonight anyway; or, Alice's friendly conversation with a person she really dislikes.

Regression is actually returning to childlike behaviors to escape demanding goals and expectations. Such behaviors include crying, sulking, temper tantrums, and sticking our tongues out at another person. Similar to displacement, regression focuses our attention away from the core issue and allows us to return to behaviors which seem more secure, again safeguarding our different selves.

As we examine our own defense mechanisms used to defend our self-systems, we should consider Hamachek's caution:

> It is worth remembering that defense mechanisms are learned adjustive behaviors, that they function on relatively unconscious levels, and that they involve a certain amount of reality distortion and self-deception. Defense mechanisms serve the aims of adjustment by reducing conflict and frustration, and particularly because they stand in guard of the self, they function as a bulwark against more serious disturbances. Consequently they can be considered quite normal and desirable, except when they are used to an excessive degree and operate at the expense of a person's ultimate adaptive efficiency and continued personal progress toward greater maturity.*

---

*From *Encounters with the Self* by Don E. Hamachek, p. 28. Copyright © 1971 by Holt, Rinehart and Winston, Inc.

Exercise 3.8

List the defense mechanisms you use in one day. Include the time, place, your actual behavior, and the reason for defending yourself. Are you using your defense mechanisms to extremes?

Day/Date: _____

Defense Mechanism	Time	Place	Actual Behavior	Reason
Projection				
Denial of reality				
Repression				
Rationalization				
Fantasy				
Compensation				
Internalization				
Displacement				
Emotional Insulation				
Reaction Formation				
Regression				

Hopefully you have not been using your defense mechanisms to dangerous extremes but have been defending the person you perceive yourself to be. Since you realize that you do incorporate defense mechanisms and assume a variety of roles during a normal day, it should be interesting to discover if others perceive the same roles and the same defense mechanisms as you do about yourself.

Exercise 3.9

For both yourself and your partner, list the roles and defense mechanisms each of you seem to use. Then compare your lists, explaining why you feel as you do about each item on your list. Were there any differences in perceptions? Why or why not? Discuss them with your partner.

Roles I Seem to Use	Defense Mechanisms I Seem to Use

Roles My Partner Seems to Use	Defense Mechanisms My Partner Seems to Use

You may want to try the exercises in this lesson with people outside your class. An important point to remember is that each person's perception of you, your roles, and your defense mechanisms will be different because of the person's different experiences with you as well as their own different experiential worlds and self-perceptions. Continually gathering information about others' perceptions of you and your perceptions of others will contribute to a better understanding of yourself and others and, therefore, to better communication. So try discussing your experiences in this lesson along with the important concepts with others, particularly those persons whom you care about.

SUMMARY

In Lesson 3, we have concentrated on the importance of learning more about our perceptions of ourselves and others. To understand and communicate more effectively with ourselves, we need to gain information about ourselves from others. Similarly, to understand and communicate more effectively with others, we need to learn how others perceive themselves and their experiential worlds. Thus, we have focused on discovering how others perceive us (and vice versa), how these perceptions were derived, and how we can increase our understanding of others' perceptions of us (and vice versa). Two dimensions influencing perceptions include roles we assume and defense mechanisms we use to maintain our self-systems. In addition, through the exercises, we have had an opportunity to examine and evaluate both our perceptions of others and others' perceptions of us.

SUGGESTIONS FOR FURTHER READING

Hamachek, Don E. *Encounters with the Self*, Chapter One, "Toward Understanding One's Self" (New York: Holt, Rinehart and Winston, 1971).

Hastorf, Albert H.; Schneider, David J.; and Polefka, Judith. *Person Perception* (Reading, Mass.: Addison-Wesley, 1970).

Stewart, John, and D'Angelo, Gary. *Together: Communicating Interpersonally*, Chapter Three, "Personal Perceiving" (Reading, Mass.: Addison-Wesley, 1975).

Tagiuri, Renato, and Petrullo, Luigi. *Person Perception and Interpersonal Behavior* (Stanford, CA.: Stanford University Press, 1958).

Wilmot, William W. *Dyadic Communication: A Transactional Perceptive*, Chapter Two, "Perception of Self" (Reading, Mass.: Addison-Wesley, 1975).

Lesson 4

Self-Understanding

Objectives

Upon completion of this lesson, you should be able to:

1. Define the following terms: self-esteem, self-acceptance, and self-disclosure.

2. Describe the characteristics of a self-accepting individual.

3. Explain in detail the relationship between perception of self and acceptance of self.

4. List and describe the methods which can be used to improve understanding of both ourselves and others.

5. Describe, analyze, and evaluate social sensitivity, active listening, and honest communication.

6. Describe the Johari Window and apply it to your own disclosure activity.

Lesson 3 stated that others' perceptions of us may not coincide with our own self-perceptions. We have also pointed out that our personal development and growth as unique individuals, and therefore, the growth and development of our self core, depends largely on our communication with others. As we interact with people from varied backgrounds and with varied perspectives, we continually gather information regarding others' perceptions of us and our perceptions of them. We thus obtain information about who we are. As communication scholars Patton and Giffin point out:

> To the extent that our personal interaction with others is successful and confirming, we are able to grow, find our identity, gain self-esteem, and feel that we are firmly in touch with reality.[36]

Most of us need other people to communicate and interact with—to reaffirm our existence as unique beings. It would be extremely difficult to face the world alone. Would you be able to get along without anyone else for an entire day? A week? A month? A year? A lifetime? I think you will agree that it would become progressively more difficult the longer we had to contend solely with ourselves.

Exercise 4.1

List the people you need to communicate with—those persons you depend on to reaffirm your existence as a unique individual.

Right now, you probably have some idea of who you are—what you are about. Are you pleased with your perceptions of yourself? If so, you undoubtedly possess a comfortable feeling of *self-esteem* or self-acceptance. Self-esteem, a term which describes one's evaluations of one's self-image, includes such feelings as confidence, adequacy, and worthiness. Patton and Giffin further define self-esteem to be one of the most important factors that makes our lives worth living. They state:

> The specific criteria for esteem may vary considerably from one person to another, but the desire for approval is almost universal. In large measure, the 'pursuit of happiness' is the pursuit of self-esteem.[37]

Perhaps you are fairly pleased with your self-perceptions but would like your "self" to be better. Do you have an ideal self in mind?

Exercise 4.2

Describe, in essay form, the person you perceive yourself to be. Are you pleased with this perception?

Day/Date: _____

Describe, in essay form, your ideal self, the person you would like to become.

Day/Date:_____

SELF-ACCEPTANCE

We have already discussed our need to communicate with others. Because of this need, and the many different people we communicate with, our feelings for each of these persons during our interactions with them will probably be a bit different also. However, basic to the feelings we have for others are the feelings we have for ourselves. That is, our self-esteem may determine our feelings about people generally, as well as determine whether we respond favorably or unfavorably to their actions toward us.[38] More specifically, our concern here is with self-acceptance or how accepting we are of our actual selves. Self-acceptance usually refers to the extent to which a person's self-concept or actual self matches the description of his or her ideal self. Don Hamachek, a well-known theorist and scholar of self-concept, explains,

> Since most of us would like to be better than we are, the *ideal* self is usually judged to be at least as good as and almost always better than the perceived or 'actual' self.*

Reexamine Exercise 4.2. Is there much discrepancy between your actual and ideal selves? Do you like your actual self? Do you approve of your actual self? Can you at least tolerate your actual self?

Because the feelings we have for ourselves are projected on to others, it is extremely important that we accept and approve of ourselves (for the most part, at least). Studies have shown that persons who are more self-accepting have higher self-concepts and show more understanding and greater acceptance of others.[39] On the other hand, those persons who dislike and reject themselves also dislike and reject others. Consider a situation in which someone disliked you, rejected you. How would you react? Eventually, you would probably dislike and reject the person, which in turn would probably reinforce the person's original behavior.[40]

Recall again Kinch's theory:[41] your behavior (rejecting the other person) would influence the others' perceptions of your behavior and thus their reactions to you. This, in turn, would influence your perceptions of yourself and consequently affect your self-concept—part of which is your acceptance of that self-concept.

Professors who recall their own inclinations to cheat on tests will glaringly oversee exams in their classrooms. In their eyes, students' behaviors represent the professors' own suppressed desire to cheat. A possible outcome of not accepting one's feelings is shown again in an example by Hamachek:

> . . . sometimes a person who feels threatened by his sexual impulses may be the first to criticize and moralize others whom he perceives as behaving in sexual ways. On the other hand, if he accepts his *own* sexual feelings he is usually more tolerant of sexual expressions by others.*

---

*From *Encounters with the Self* by Don E. Hamachek, p. 230. Copyright © 1971 by Holt, Rinehart and Winston, Inc. Adapted by permission of Holt, Rinehart and Winston.

Why should one's perception of oneself affect his or her perceptions of other people? Taking into account how self-concept develops (refer to Lessons 1 and 2), complete Exercise 4.3.

Exercise 4.3

Present several reasons that would explain why acceptance of self and acceptance for others are so closely related.

Do you recall our discussion of reflected appraisal in Lesson 2? Reflected appraisal refers to using other people as a mirror to reflect our behavior. When David, age seven, receives continuous hostility from significant people in his life—his parents, his brothers and sisters, his classmates—a negative reaction to himself is likely to develop. As he learns to dislike himself, he also develops a dislike for his parents, his siblings, and his peers. A general dislike for other people may follow from his early experiences with these reflected appraisals from significant people. Reflected appraisal, then, is one possible reason for the close relationship between acceptance of self and acceptance of others.

Another explanation for the relationship between self-acceptance and acceptance of others suggests that the person who feels inferior (low self-esteem) may not wish to admit to himself or herself that others have positive attributes: "If I'm not good at creative writing, no one is." Acknowledging others' superior qualities makes us feel worse, since we tend to compare ourselves with them. However, if we see others as inferior, we boost our own self-esteem (see Figure 4.1). (Refer to the discussion of social comparison in Lessons 2 and 3.)

Through selecting information we wish to see and hear about others (*selective perception*), we can always find shortcomings or negative attributes in others. In this way, we prove to ourselves we are not so bad after all.

Finally, we generally assume other people are like ourselves, particularly if we don't know them very well. We make this mistake more often when we *think* we know the other person well. For example, when discussing the latest musical styles with a friend, we are amazed when he or she doesn't approve of the same artists as we do. Similarly, if we do not accept some of our own qualities, we will reject those same qualities in others.

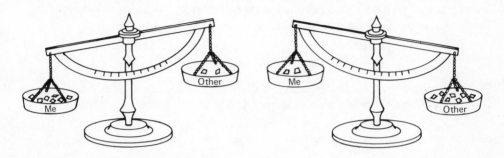

Figure 4.1. Relationship between self-acceptance and other-acceptance. If we give others negative points, *our* self-esteem increases.

Consider Julia's case. Because Julia has been rejected in the past and believes she has no friends, she expects and therefore selectively perceives negative responses (verbal and nonverbal) when she interacts with people. Her low self-esteem is reinforced by her actions. She believes she is inadequate in social relationships and therefore gives up before allowing a friendship to develop.

The same progression of events occurs for the self-accepting person. Ron, who assumes others are like him, accepts and approves of himself and, therefore, selectively perceives positive reactions in his interactions with others. Again, his positive self-esteem is reinforced by his actions. He takes time to meet new people, to talk to and to listen to them, and accepts them for the persons they are. Ron's acceptance of others encourages their acceptance of him, which reinforces his original behavior.

As Figure 4.2 indicates, effective communication requires understanding and acceptance of both oneself and others. Understanding ourselves provides

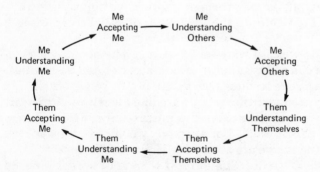

Figure 4.2. A model of effective communication.

the basis for our acceptance of ourselves; similarly, understanding others pro-
motes acceptance of others. In fact, self and other understanding provides
specific knowledge about how each person's unique individuality grows and
develops in an interpersonal communication situation. William Brooks, noted
speech communication author, states:

> . . . we must receive information from others so as to gain a greater
> understanding of self, and we must share ourselves with others.[42]

Three ingredients, if incorporated into our self-systems as we communicate with others, should help enhance our understanding of our different
selves and of others. They are social sensitivity, active listening, and honest
communication. As each is discussed, reflect on your own behaviors in your
communication with others.

SOCIAL SENSITIVITY

It is important to empathize with one another; to see, to feel, and to hear
with the other person.[43] Social sensitivity implies going beyond our own personal motivations in an attempt to understand the other person's feelings,
thoughts, needs, and goals. It means forgetting about ourselves for the
moment and stepping into the other person's shoes, to fully understand that
person. We need to examine our different selves from a different perspective—
from the other person's world. By becoming less involved with ourselves, we
can be more objective about ourselves. By sharing mutual concerns, we can discover how and why others perceive the world as they do. Social sensitivity,
then, is an attempt to understand ourselves through understanding others. To
maximize our social sensitivity, however, we should incorporate active listening into our communication systems.

ACTIVE LISTENING

Active listening demands our total commitment to communication. It requires much more than just waiting until the other person finishes his or her
statement. Active listening requires us to try to view the world as seen by the
other person and to communicate this understanding to him or her. As
Hamachek suggests, this kind of listening

> . . . implies no evaluation, no judgment, no agreement (or disagreement).
> It simply conveys an effort to understand what the person is feeling and
> trying to communicate.[44]

To respond to a person's feelings, we must consider the other person's
verbal and nonverbal communication. Nonverbal communication includes
tone of voice, rate of speech, facial and eye expressions, gestures, posture,
spatial distance—the intangible cues which complement the verbal message.
We must listen between the lines with all our senses to fully understand the other
person.

With active listening, we communicate our acceptance of the other person along with acceptance of his or her ideas, attitudes, and values. Even though we may not agree with these ideas, attitudes, and/or values, we can still accept and appreciate these dimensions as part of the person we are communicating with.

Active listening is not easy, especially when we disagree with the other person. How many times we have failed to register and interpret the other person's message without immediate evaluation?

Have you ever tried to paraphrase what someone has said to you, satisfying the person that what you said is what he or she meant? As communication scholars, Stewart and D'Angelo point out, *paraphrasing* is saying in your own words " . . . how you've interpreted the other person's ideas and feelings."[45] It's not repeating the other person's comment word for word; rather, it's an attempt to communicate your understanding of both what the person said and how he or she feels about it. Paraphrasing is not always easy. In the following example, Ken paraphrases Rich's statement:

Rich: Man, this class really stinks.

Ken: Sounds like you're not getting what you expected out of this course.

Rich: Nah, not exactly. I just can't keep up with all the assignments.

In the preceding example, if Ken just said, "Sounds like you don't like the class," he probably would not have received Rich's further explanation of what he meant by "this class really stinks." In Exercise 4.4, try out your own listening and paraphrasing skills.

Exercise 4.4

With two friends, designate one another as Person A, Person B, and Person C. Person A should begin talking to B about anything in which A is interested (sports, politics, the educational system, dating protocol in today's society, etc.). Person B should paraphrase and communicate back to A what A has said—to A's complete satisfaction. Person C should observe the interaction and check on the agreement between A's original message and B's paraphrasing. If, at any time, there is dissatisfaction with B's feedback message, A should clarify the original message, with B rephrasing the clarification. When agreement has been reached between A's message and B's response, and all are satisfied with the understanding of the message, switch roles: B becomes A; C becomes B; and A becomes C. Then switch again so the Person C will have an opportunity to originate a message. A then becomes B and B becomes C.

When you have completed the exercise, list and discuss the difficulties, if any, your group had in obtaining agreement between the message sent and the message received. If there were difficulties, what do you think are the reasons for them?

Perhaps your group did not perceive any problems in gaining agreement between the message sent and the message received. If you did have difficulties, what caused them? Examine your communication interactions in general. What causes misunderstandings between the message sent and the message received?

Did your mind wander from the subject? Why? Perhaps you found yourself responding to what you thought you heard? Or to what you wanted to hear? Refer to our discussion in Lesson 1 about our selectivity in perception, decoding, evaluation, and integration of incoming information. Was it operating in your communication with others? To be truly active listeners, we need to hear and listen to what a person is actually saying, rather then racing through our own experiential world to sift, interpret, and evaluate the stored information related to the other person's topic.

Sometimes, while the other person is speaking, we think about the person. As listening theorist Allan Katcher suggests:

> We try to evaluate the worth of his words, seek for deep motivation, and make judgments about the person and what he is saying, rather than understanding what he is saying, rather than understanding where he is.[46]

Perhaps we race ahead in our thoughts, formulating our own ideas, criticizing, summarizing, and coming to conclusions about the intended message before the person has finished; in essence, we think for the other person, often completing his or her statement ourselves. This kind of response leaves little room for truly understanding the other person, or ourselves. Although we may have relevant and meaningful things to say, we may actually be afraid to actively listen to the other person for fear that person may wish to change our ideas about the topic of conversation.

Because active listening requires our total commitment to the person communicating, we necessarily become open to new and different ideas, attitudes, and values. This forces us to examine and question our own ideas, attitudes, and values. We then become vulnerable to change. Since our ideas, attitudes, and values help comprise our self-concept core, opening ourselves to changes through active listening often produces uncertainty. Yet, at the same time, through this unselfish giving of ourselves, through this total listening, we begin to learn more about the other person, understand him or her better, and become more accepting of him or her. All of our giving and accepting then returns to us, creating a better understanding and acceptance of ourselves.

As you can see, social sensitivity and active listening are tightly intertwined. We need to combine both in our communication with others. For complete understanding of ourselves and others, however, honest communication is a prerequisite.

HONEST COMMUNICATION

Honest communication does not suggest, as Hamachek says, becoming "brutally and indiscriminately frank" with our friends (or enemies). Rather, it implies exposing some of ourselves to another person, expressing some of our own ideas, feelings, and attitudes.[47] From our earliest interactions, we have been taught to hide our true, honest feelings by not saying things to others which could potentially hurt them—or us. Honest communication, however, requires removing the defense mechanisms which suppress our feelings (as we discussed in Lesson 3). Admittedly, brutal and indiscriminate frankness will not promote increased understanding or acceptance for either the sender or receiver. However, we can begin to promote our own self-development and our understanding of ourselves and others by allowing our feelings to emerge more often than they have before.

Our roles in society place heavy burdens on the ways we express our emotions. Males learn early not to cry. Although females are permitted to express their emotions through crying, they learn not to curse. We should not necessarily change our roles. Rather, we should recognize our feelings, accept them, and share them with someone.

By exposing and sharing feelings with others, we can develop an even closer interpersonal relationship. As I share part of myself with you, I communicate my trust in you, and encourage you to trust me and share your feelings with me. We learn about one another; we learn to better understand and accept one another and ourselves.

Exercise 4.5

Try to share some feelings with someone, some feelings about a pleasant experience and the emotions you felt during and after your experience. After completing your sharing, answer the following questions.

1. Describe, in detail, how you felt telling this person about your experience.

2. Describe, in detail, how you felt telling this person about your feelings.

3. What was your overall reaction to this sharing experience?

SELF-DISCLOSURE

Honest communication is further facilitated by self-disclosure. Although similar to sharing our feelings, self-disclosure progresses a bit further in communicating ourselves to others. Self-disclosure means to share with another person some personal information which the other person could not possibly learn from anyone else.[48] It does not mean telling the deep dark secrets of our past. Secrets may become disclosures, but the true purpose of self-disclosure is learning more about ourselves through our relationship with the other person.

> When you share something of what is presently going on in you, you show in a concrete way your desire to become involved with the other persons present on more than a superficial level.[49]

There are many things we might disclose to one another. Communication writer John Keltner lists such disclosure items as attitudes and opinions, tastes and interests, work perceptions, money perceptions, physical likes and dislikes (bodily activities), self-perceptions, feelings and perceptions of each other and others, personality choices, loves and hates, fears and anxieties, and even reactions to this moment.[50]

For example, you've hidden your fear and anxiety about speaking in front of a group of people. Upon disclosing this to at least one other person, you may be suprised to discover that this person also has this same fear. Some of the greatest actors and actresses still get nervous on opening night. Your professor probably also felt anxious the first time he or she walked into your classroom this semester. It's a natural feeling when we're not sure what to expect. In addition, the other person may not perceive your anxiousness at all; in fact, he or she might have perceived you as cool and calm when you've spoken in front of other people. Because so many of us hate to admit (or perhaps have just learned to hold inside) our feelings, we never learn about others' feelings and, consequently, never learn more about ourselves.

Both our self-disclosures and a simple sharing of our feelings, however, need to be appropriate to the situation in which we're involved and our relationship with the other individual.[51] Good self-disclosures help to improve our growth and development as unique individuals, enhancing our intrapersonal communication. Therefore, a random disclosure to a stranger on a bus would not be classified as a self-growth disclosure; the disclosure would be appropriate neither to the situation (riding on a crowded bus) nor to your relationship with the individual (a stranger).

To use self-disclosures most appropriately and to their fullest potential, we should remember several points. First of all, self-disclosures should be made only in a setting of good will and trust. Because there is a degree of risk with any self-disclosure, we must be able to trust the individual to whom we are disclosing. It means making an investment in the other person.[52]

In the past, you may have shared and disclosed information about yourself to a friend because you felt that he or she was trustworthy and would not reveal certain personal information to others. It was a private matter, but you wanted to share it with someone. Perhaps your confidant did not realize the personal nature of your disclosure and told it to someone else. Soon, your message returned via a different source altogether. And it hurt. It hurt so badly, you intended never to speak to that person or share any information about yourself again. Who could blame you? Our only consolation, perhaps, is that it has happened to most of us.

Second, self-disclosure involves risk. Why then should we risk part of ourselves? Because it helps our personal growth and development. Of course, we should be in full control of when, what, how much and to whom we disclose. Therefore, we should choose our self-disclosure partners carefully. The individual should be someone whom we care about and with whom we want to further our interpersonal relationship. Also, the information we decide to share should be relevant to our relationship with the other person, helping him or her learn about our feelings and attitudes toward mutual concerns. The time and place also have a bearing on our disclosures: we need more than five minutes and most likely a place away from a crowd of people.

Third, before we can disclose information about ourselves, we obviously need to know it about ourselves first. In a diagram developed by Joseph Luft and Harrington Ingram, termed the Johari Window (note Johari comprises both men's names: Joe and Harry), we can see more clearly our different disclosure patterns (see figure 4.3). We can assume we possess a different Johari Window for each person with whom we communicate.

Area I, or the *free area*, includes information known to both ourselves and others. The information in this window comprises those things which we are willing to share with the other person: age, major, home location, favorite foods, etc.

Area II is labeled the *blind area*, because it includes information others know about us which we do not know about ourselves. For example, there are things about others (perhaps nonverbal behaviors) of which you are aware and they are not. Those persons who chew on their pens, those who tap their feet, or those who never establish eye contact with us may not know these things about themselves.

A student of mine never realized she laughed whenever she became nervous. Even when discussing extremely serious problems, Kate would chuckle (her nervous reaction), annoying her friends who considered her behavior intolerable. Because a close friend disclosed to Kate her behavior (information in Kate's blind area), Kate is now aware of it and explains her behavior before it becomes embarrasing. Her nervous laughter is now a part of Kate's free area.

Area III, or the *hidden area*, contains information which we know about ourselves but which we keep hidden from others. This information is ripe for disclosure, since only we know the contents of this window. For

	Known to Self	Not Known to Self
Known to Others	I Free Area	II Blind Area
Not Known to Others	III Hidden Area	IV Unknown Area

Figure 4.3. The Johari Window. Reprinted from *Of Human Action* by Joseph Luft with permission of Mayfield Publishing Company (formerly National Press Books). Copyright © 1969 by The National Press.

example, I may be complaining to a friend about how much I dislike a particular course, but never reveal that I failed three of the four tests. Disclosing this information would help to clarify my feelings, helping the other person to understand my discontent.

Area IV is classified as the *unknown area*, because neither we nor others know the information located here. For example, while at a friend's apartment, John picked up a guitar. He had never played before, but he began to strum the strings. His friend, who was quite talented, commented that John should take lessons since he seemed to be a natural guitar player. With his friend's help, John discovered something about himself which neither he nor his friend knew before.

With each separate listener, we communicate with a totally different Johari Window. In our interactions with a professor, for example, our Johari Window may look like this:

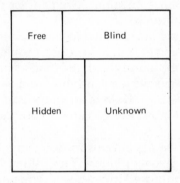

While we are in communication with a parent or friend, our Johari Window may look like this:

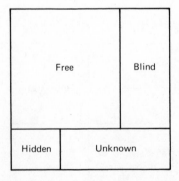

For developing and growing as unique persons in our communication with others, then, our task is to widen our open areas and tighten our hidden areas through self-disclosure. Simultaneously, no doubt, our blind and unknown areas will also shrink, thus allowing us to develop a better understanding of ourselves. This process leads to effective communication. (Refer back to the illustration of effective communication on p. 76.)

Fourth, the words we use are crucial to the total effectiveness of our disclosures. Communication scholars Stewart and D'Angelo strongly urge that the words we employ in our disclosures include:

> . . . first-person pronouns, present tense, active voice, concrete specifics, and the language of the present experience.[53]

We should communicate our disclosures to our partner by focusing on the specifics of our feelings at the present time. The following are some fairly simple rules to follow in your disclosures.[54]

I Rule: Talking in terms of yourself; personalizing your conversation with yourself. The following list of lead-ins may help you use this rule:

I feel . . .
My opinion is . . .
I believe . . .
To me it is . . .
For myself . . .
I think . . .

Understanding Response: Reflecting back in your own words the ideas, thoughts, or feelings stated by the other person. (*Note:* This is similar to our discussion on paraphrasing.) The following phrases may help you get started with the understanding response:

What you seem to be saying is . . .
I think you're saying . . .
From what you've just said, it seems that you mean . . .

Who Rule: Talking directly to, not about, a person with respect to your perceptions of his or her behavior. The following lead-ins may help you utilize this rule:

I feel that you are . . .
I see you as . . .
You seem to be the kind of person who . . .

Exercise 4.6

This exercise is optional. Because this is the first exercise in self-disclosure, you should select a partner carefully. Choose someone you would like to get to know better, someone you feel you can trust. You are in control of this exercise, since you determine what, how much, and to whom you will disclose. Use the suggestions given in this section. Although this is an exercise [55] and for that reason not completely realistic, it will still provide you with experience in using the rules for self-disclosure.

Procedure

1.   Once you have a partner, each person will alternate using the words provided later in this exercise and describe himself or herself in terms of these words. For this portion, be sure to use the *I rule* and be as specific as possible. For example, with the word, happiness, I would begin by saying, "To me, happiness is . . .," or "I feel happiness is . . .". etc.

2.   After one member has completed his or her description, the other partner should respond using the *understanding response*. For example, after I describe what happiness is to me, you would say "What you seem to be saying is that for you, happiness is . . .."

3.   At three points during the exercise, each person will practice using the *who rule* by directly describing his or her reactions toward the other person, being as specific as possible.

4.   Decide whether you want an observer. Two possibilities are:

   a.   Each participant should be aware of the rules and make sure the rules are followed by both participants.

   b.   Each pair of participants should have an observer, whose primary role will be to make sure the rules are followed. The observer allows the participants to concentrate fully on listening and responding to one another. The observer is not an intruder but rather an aid in carrying out the exercise.

Use *I rule* and *understanding response:* Describe yourself in terms of the following words.

Happiness:

Dislike:

Rejection:

Strengths:

Affection:

Use *who rule:* As a result of our conversation so far, I feel you are a person who . . .

Use *I rule* and *understanding response:* Describe yourself in terms of the following words.

Mistakes:

Friendship:

Prejudices:

Loneliness:

Frustration:

Use *who rule:* I feel we are similar in that you are . . . and I am . . . .

I feel we are different in that you are . . . and I am . . . .

Use *I rule* and *understanding response:* Describe yourself in terms of the following words:

Unhappiness:

Love:

Anxieties:

Belonging:

Use *who rule:* After having this experience with you, I feel you are . . ..

After having this experience with you, I feel I am . . . .

Exercise 4.7

Since you have had an opportunity to experience self-disclosure, how did you feel? Describe your reactions to this exercise in as much detail as possible, using the *I rule*.

Exercise 4.8

Showing approximate areas for each window pane, draw a Johari Window for your relationship to your partner and your partner's relationship to you both before and after Exercise 4.6. Refer back to the example with the professor on page 84, where our initial interactions may have been:

Free	Blind
Hidden	Unknown

Our interactions after a conference with the same professor may be:

Free	Blind
Hidden	Unknown

My Johari Window with

_____
(partner's name)

_____'s
(partner's name)

Johari Window with me

Before:

After:

Exercise 4.9

As an aid to further self-understanding and self-development, this exercise
will help you to categorize your disclosure activity for the rest of the semester. In a notebook, label the appropriate headings of the Johari Window
and keep track of your disclosures using the following list of topics (and
any others you wish). If you learn something new about yourself, be sure
to add it to your list, determining whether it is known to others or not. As
you disclose information originally listed in Area III, your hidden area, to at
least one other person, cross it off and add it to Area I, your free area. Also,
keep a record of information which others disclose to you about yourself
(you may want to put their names next to the disclosure items). This process will help you obtain a fuller understanding of your intrapersonal self.

Self-Disclosure Topics*

1. Your favorite foods and beverages; your least-liked foods and beverages.
2. Favorite hobbies, sports, pastimes; least-liked activities.
3. Music you prefer; music you dislike.
4. Best times of your college day; worst times. Best times of your day
   away from college; worst times.
5. How you feel about higher education generally; your college/university
   specifically; your educational background.
6. Your perceptions about your future—five years from now; ten years
   from now.
7. Goals for this week; goals for this year.
8. Characteristics of a good friend; name(s) of person(s) you would consider to be your best friend(s).
9. The educational and family background of your parents.
10. Aspects you like most about your family; like least.
11. Your personal views on politics (local, national, international), the
    economy, the environment.
12. Your religious views (if any). Your parent's religious views (if any).
13. Your feelings about where you live; how you live; your socioeconomic
    status.
14. The happiest moments in your life, in detail.
15. The unhappiest moments in your life, in detail.

*From *The Transparent Self* by Sidney Jourard © 1971 by Litton Educational Publishing Inc. Reprinted by permission of D. Van Nostrand Company.

16. Personal characteristics or qualities of which you are extremely pleased and proud.

17. Personal characteristics or qualities which bother you; things you would like to improve or change.

18. Your fantasies, unfulfilled wishes, desires, dreams.

19. The times you feel you've failed.

20. The times you feel you've succeeded.

21. The usual methods you use to deal with your loneliness, depression, anger.

22. The situations in which you become depressed, annoyed, ecstatic, giggly.

23. The circumstances which lead to your feelings being hurt.

24. Ways you like to show affection, love, friendship.

25. The ways in which you feel you are most immature.

26. Defense mechanisms you often use.

27. Mistakes you've made in your life.

28. Mistakes your parents have made in raising you.

29. Your perceptions of your parents' relationship with you; with one another.

30. Health problems you have now or have had in the past.

31. Health problems of your family, your closest friend(s).

32. Your relationship with the opposite sex.

33. Friends' behaviors of which you disapprove.

34. Those aspects of your appearance you are most pleased with; most displeased with.

35. Methods you use to stay physically fit (if any).

36. People whom you most admire; your reasons why.

37. People who have played a significant role in your life, in detail.

38. People whom you dislike; your reasons why.

39. Places you've traveled to; places you would like to visit, live.

Your own topics?

Remember, we control our disclosures. We do not and should not tell everyone everything about ourselves. Rather, if we can tell at least one other person something we haven't told anyone before, we have an opportunity to receive feedback about our behaviors and our perceptions of ourselves. This feedback will further clarify the elements of our self-concept core, enabling more effective intrapersonal communication.

SUMMARY

Lesson 4 provided information and exercises for promoting understanding of ourselves and others. To fully understand ourselves and others, acceptance of both ourselves and others is necessary because of the intimate connection between them for total and effective communication. Social sensitivity, active listening, and honest communication were discussed as three important elements that should be incorporated into our self-systems for improved self-other understanding and improved intrapersonal and interpersonal communication.

SUGGESTIONS FOR FURTHER READING

Culbert, Samuel A. *The Interpersonal Process of Self-Disclosure: It Takes Two to See One* (New York: Renaissance Editions, 1968).

Johnson, David W. *Reaching Out* (Englewood Cliffs, N.J. Prentice-Hall, 1972).

Jourard, Sidney M. *The Transparent Self* revised ed. (New York: Van Nostrand Reinhold, 1971).

Katcher, Allan. "Self-Fulfilling Prophecies and Active Listening," in John Stewart, ed., *Bridges Not Walls: A Book About Interpersonal Communication* (Reading Mass.: Addison-Wesley, 1973).

Luft, Joseph. *Of Human Interaction* (Palo Alto, Cal.: National Press, 1969).

Lesson 5

Self-Enhancement

Objectives

Upon completion of this lesson, you should be able to:

1. Define an enhanced self-concept.

2. Explain how self-concept can be modified.

3. List, explain, and implement the six guidelines for self-enhancement.

4. Describe, develop, and implement a plan for your own self-enhancement.

Self-concept includes perceptions, ideas, attitudes, and evaluations a person has of himself or herself (physically, socially, and intellectually).

Throughout this book, our emphasis has been on self-concept as the core of our communication processing. Our self-concept (or self-image; or perception of ourselves) influences our behavior and our interactions with others, which, in turn, influence others' reactions toward us. Because our communication with others is crucial to our total development as human beings, and since self-concept is an inseparable link in the communication connection, our efforts should be directed to improving and enhancing our perceptions of ourselves.

Self-concept enhancement, however, does not imply that we assume the identity of Captain Marvel, Superwoman, or some other invincible personality. Rather, possessing an enhanced self-concept means we perceive ourselves objectively and accurately, *accepting* both our strengths and weaknesses. More simply, self-concept enhancement means we feel good about ourselves; we feel good about who we are.

As Lesson 2 suggested, however, that self-concept is extremely difficult to change, primarily because each of us has a basic need to maintain the self we perceive—to stay just the way we are. We desire to maintain consistent ideas, attitudes, and values developed from our past experiences, which are retained in our experiential world. We continually strive to defend our self-image and to confirm it in the presence of others. Again, we accomplish our task of preserving our different selves through selective perception: seeing, hearing, and thinking only those things which essentially agree with the ideas, attitudes, and values we already hold. We also rely on our selected roles and our defense mechanisms to help maintain the self.

Past studies of self-concept, however, prove self-concept can be modified to a certain degree.[56] The image or concept we have of ourselves—our adequacy, personal worth, and confidence—can be enhanced. Lesson 2 demonstrated that the attitudes we have about ourselves are primarily learned through our interactions with others, particularly significant people. Perhaps we have learned negative or self-defeating attitudes about ourselves. To change our concepts of ourselves, then, we need to replace those negative attitudes with healthier, positive attitudes. As Hamachek clearly explains, although "we cannot change past experiences, . . . we can change our feelings about those experiences . . . ."[57]

In an effort to change our feelings about negative experiences, and thus enhance our perceptions of ourselves—enhance our intrapersonal core—we can follow six guidelines. These six guidelines have been tested and evaluated and have proven beneficial in promoting self-concept enhancement. Based on experimental and theoretical research conducted on self-concept theory, the guidelines include suggestions and exercises for an individualized self-enhancement program.[58] The program concludes with general suggestions for all communication interactions.

SIX GUIDELINES FOR AN ENHANCED SELF-CONCEPT

Guideline 1: Evaluate Yourself Realistically

An initial step toward enhancing our own self-concept is to determine how we evaluate our many selves. Lesson 2 showed how our self-concept is determined for the most part by our evaluating ourselves in terms of others' perceptions of us. We assess our ideas, attitudes, and values by comparing them with others' ideas, attitudes, and values. As young children, we depend heavily on others' reactions and evaluations of us; however, as we grow and mature, we accept more of the responsibility for our self-evaluation.

At times, however, some of us become too zealous in our quest for truth; we become overly critical. This is especially true in our evaluations of ourselves. Others of us, on the other hand, are too easy on ourselves and noncritically accept all of our qualities and abilities. Although it may appear contradictory to our discussion on self-acceptance, our goal for an enhanced self-concept should be *objective realism*. We need to find the middle ground between being too critical and not critical enough in our self-evaluations. According to Coopersmith[59] and LaBenne and Greene,[60] noted researchers in self-concept theory, we should examine our different selves—our abilities, skills, characteristics—and evaluate them realistically.

Although it is not always easy to be objective and realistic in our evaluations, we obtain a clearer picture of our different selves as we continue to grow and mature. To aid us in examining ourselves realistically, two self-evaluation inventories are provided. Exercise 5.1 focuses on strengths, while Exercise 5.2 examines thos qualities and characteristics which need improvement.

Did you discover your strong points through your disclosure exercises in Lesson 4? Try to include all your strong points in Exercise 5.1, updating the list as you discover others. To begin, you may want to consult the following categories:

Physical characteristics: Do you have nice eyes? Hair? Good posture? Cute toes? Soft skin? List all of your strong and positive attributes.

Physical abilities: Are you good at sports? Which ones? How about dancing? Sewing? Painting? Fixing things? Cleaning? Cooking? Gardening? Remember, be specific.

Mental abilities: Are you good with numbers? Ideas? Practical logic? Organizing thoughts? Academic subjects? Nonacademic subjects?

Social attributes: Are you a good conversationalist? Active listener? Good public speaker? Good leader? Group participant? Do you use language effectively? Make friends easily? Interact easily with others? Make others feel comfortable? Do things on your own well? Love other persons: parents, siblings, special friends?

Personal characteristics: Are you cheerful? Thoughtful? Understanding? Helpful? Enthusiastic? Flexible? Even tempered? Loyal?

Exercise 5.1

List your strengths, providing specific details of each of your strong points. For example, if you're generally good at tennis, explain exactly what you feel your strengths are: forehand, backhand, serve, etc. While listing your strengths, you should also evaluate each: 6 = Superior; 5 = Excellent; and 4 = Good. Also, check (√) your reaction to your specific strengths indicating their importance to you. Remember, the goal is to be both objective and realistic in our evaluations. Use additional pages if necessary.

Inventory of Strengths

Strength	Evaluation				
	Importance to Me				
	Extremely Important	*Important*	*Neutral*	*Unimportant*	*Extremely Unimportant*

Strength   **Evaluation**

	Importance to Me				
	Extremely Important	*Important*	*Neutral*	*Unimportant*	*Extremely Unimportant*

Exercise 5.2

List those abilities, qualities, and characteristics which you feel need improvement. You may use the same categories as provided for your "Inventory of Strengths," including others if you wish. Indicate your *evaluation* of the improvement area and its importance: 3 = Needs little improvement; 2 = Needs some improvement; 1 = Needs much improvement. Again, the goal is to be both objective and realistic in our evaluations. Use additional pages if necessary.

Inventory of Improvement Areas

Area of Improvement   Evaluation

	Importance to Me				
	Extremely Important	*Important*	*Neutral*	*Unimportant*	*Extremely Unimportant*

**Area of
Improvement**   Evaluation

	Importance to Me				
	Extremely Important	*Important*	*Neutral*	*Unimportant*	*Extremely Unimportant*

Guideline 2: Set Realistic Goals

Through realistic and honest self-evaluations, we can objectively perceive our strengths and weaknesses. Obviously, to enhance our self-concept, we have to feel good about ourselves. If, through our honest appraisal of ourselves, we're disappointed with particular characteristics or attributes we possess, then we should concentrate on improving those weaker areas. This is necessary for a fully functioning, enhanced self. It is important to remember, however, that each of us has certain limitations in our physical, social, and intellectual capabilities. We can't all be good at everything; each of us is unique and has different strengths. However, we can improve ourselves to a certain extent. The most efficient method for accomplishing self-improvement is to set realistic goals, which will maximize our successes and minimize our failures in specific endeavors.[61]

Realistic goals imply specifying outcomes which are neither too high nor too low. Consider the following example. Entering college as a freshman, Alice decides she wants to be a corporate president within fifteen years. Although this is an admirable goal, Alice has not considered her capabilities (as of now, she knows nothing about the business world), nor has she been very realistic in setting her goal. This situation would not help Alice obtain self-acceptance or an enhanced self-concept.

Alice's first goal should be to complete several business courses to determine whether she truly desires that field, and does well in it. Then she can obtain a degree which will give her a firm background for corporate business. With this approach, Alice will feel good about succeeding each time she reaches a realistic goal. Then she will be able to set another realistic goal, based on what she knows about her abilities. Alice may discover she is quite satisfied in an organizational development and planning position in which she does quite well, or she may find business is not her field.

Although goals set too low are not as damaging as those set too high, they still do not provide the necessary enhancement for our self-concept. They do not carry the same impact as realistic goals because they are accomplished too easily. Winning a card game of War isn't as rewarding or self-satisfying as winning at Bridge or Poker; it isn't as challenging.

When designing realistic goals, we should keep in mind several additional suggestions. First, goals should be clearly defined.[62] When deciding on the goals we will pursue, we should carefully consider (preferably write down) exactly what we want to accomplish. When we know our specific goal, we will then be able to determine the necessary abilities required for the goal, as well as the steps we will need to accomplish the goal.

Second, goals should be flexible.[63] We should not commit ourselves to a goal with an "all or nothing" philosophy; rather, we should allow ourselves the option to modify or change a goal if we so desire. Flexible goals provide more success. Rather than degrading ourselves for not reaching a goal, we can still feel good about ourselves when we change a goal, because we realized the necessity for change. A person who has extreme difficulty in grasping the basic concepts in mathematics and physics should probably not try to become a physicist—not yet, at any rate. Instead, the goal should be modified.

Third, goals should be meaningful, yet challenging.[64] The basic reason for setting realistic goals is to be able to feel success once we've achieved the desired outcome. However, if the initial goal is not meaningful, or if the goal is too easily accomplished, it will not contain the desired impact for self-concept enhancement. On the other hand, when a personally meaningful goal, which also challenges one's abilities, is attained, self-esteem should grow.

Guideline 3: Concentrate on Improvement, Not Perfection

Although this third guideline for enhancing our self-concept relates closely to our first two guidelines, it is extremely important and rates separate consideration. Both in evaluating ourselves and in setting our goals, we should focus specifically on how we can improve, not how we can become perfect.[65] Perfection (no matter how good we are at something) is always beyond us. When we set our sights on perfection and then do not attain it, we experience failure, rather than a potential success if we tried for improvement. This is not to suggest that failure should be avoided at all costs, but we need to learn from our mistakes, and concentrate on improvement, not perfection.

Exercise 5.3

This exercise will help you rank in order those areas you wish to work on for your self-enhancement program. Reexamine Exercise 5.2 where you've listed those characteristics and abilities you would like to improve. Circle those areas which are extremely important to you. Of those you've circled, list those which have a score of 3 (needs little improvement) in the appropriate space. Continue the same procedure for the remaining categories.

Category I

Score = 3: Needs Little Improvement

Extremely
Important
Areas for
Improvement

Category II

Score = 2: Needs Some Improvement

Extremely
Important
Areas for
Improvement

Category III

Score = 1: Needs Much Improvement

Extremely
Important
Areas for
Improvement

Category IV

Score = 3: Needs Little Improvement

Important
Areas for
Improvement

Category V

Score = 2: Needs Some Improvement

Important
Areas for
Improvement

Category VI

Score = 1: Needs Much Improvement

Important
Areas for
Improvement

As you undoubtedly noticed, the exercise you've just completed provides an ordering of those areas of self-improvement which you consider important. By beginning with the areas which need little improvement, you will probably obtain success in reaching your initial goals. Now continue to Exercise 5.4.

Exercise 5.4

In this exercise, you can determine which goals you wish to work on and design your plan for accomplishing them. Begin by selecting only one area from Category I: Extremely Important/Needs Little Improvement. Once you have decided on an area, list it in Column 1. Then, *carefully* determine the goal(s) which you wish to pursue for that area and list them in Column 2. (Remember to use the suggestions for designing realistic goals.) Next, fill in Column 3, indicating the abilities, qualities, etc. which are necessary to accomplish the goal, If you possess the necessary basic competencies, continue to Column 5 to determine the steps you will need to take to attain your general goal. You will find each step will probably become an additional goal in itself.

You may need to use a notebook for this exercise since the space available here is limited.

Do not hesitate to modify your goal (or the steps to reach your goal) as you deem necessary. Your task is to reach success and feel good about yourself. Follow the suggestions for determining realistic goals which will help you achieve success and minimize failure in your endeavor.

Remember, complete only one area at a time.

As you continue planning your self-enhancement program, proceed with the ordering of your improvement areas in Exercise 5.3. You may want to consult a friend for feedback on your plan. Hopefully, you have selected objective and realistic goals which you can accomplish in time, thus providing successful outcomes and a more enhanced self.

Column 1	Column 2	Column 3	Column 4	Column 5
Improvement Area	Goal	Necessary Abilities	Do I Have the Required Abilities?	Necessary Steps to Accomplish Goal: In Detail

Column 1	Column 2	Column 3	Column 4	Column 5
Improvement Area	Goal	Necessary Abilities	Do I Have the Required Abilities?	Necessary Steps to Accomplish Goal: In Detail

Exercise 5.5

Having listed all the necessary steps for the accomplishment of at least one goal in Exercise 5.4, begin to implement your plan. What are the first steps you need to take? Follow your plan methodically, modifying your pro- cedures when necessary. Try not to become frustrated if the process pro- ceeds more slowly than you anticipated. Your plan will take time; changing the characteristics which have been part of your self and experiential world (perhaps for years) cannot be changed overnight. You may be able to work on more than one goal at a time but be careful not to rush the process.

Now that you have designed your goals and the procedures to imple- ment them, there is one specific guideline which needs to be incorporated for a fully developed self-concept enhancement program.

Guideline 4: Praise Yourself

This is perhaps the most important of all the guidelines to enhancing self- concept. We've already discussed the implications of self-acceptance on our interactions with others (Lesson 4): the more accepting we are of ourselves, the more we understand and accept others; this leads to others' understand- ing and accepting themselves and, consequently, to their understanding and accepting us. A 1970 study conducted by Felker and Bahlke[66] found posi- tive self-evaluation in the form of verbal reinforcements to be positively related to the individual's self-concept. Instead of quietly accepting our strong points, we need to let others know we are pleased with ourselves, whatever the quality or ability is.

Having analyzed and listed our strong points for Guideline 1, we should now tell others about them. We often hesitate to praise ourselves, however, because our society frowns on our complimenting ourselves or accepting praise from others. Instead, we degrade ourselves so we don't appear to brag. Do the following dialogues sound familiar?

Sue: Gee, Anna, you really look good today.

Anna: Ah, na I don't. I've had these clothes for years.

or:

Tim: Jimmy, you run track like a pro— that was excellent time!

Jimmy: Well, maybe. But I could have done better.

Many people in today's society are afraid to admit they look good, feel good, or have done something well. We should accept ourselves—accept our strengths and communicate that acceptance to ourselves and others: *out loud!*

In Exercises 5.6 and 5.7, you will have an opportunity to praise yourself in front of someone else. You may be suprised at the positive reactions you'll receive. Here's one example:

Ailanna: You know Jill, I'm really pleased with my progress in math; I never realized I could be good at it.

Jill: I agree, Ailanna, you've done very well. Have you ever considered tutoring others in math?

As long as your evaluation of yourself is realistic, you'll find that others will begin to respect your honesty and your self-acceptance and will probably take on similar behaviors. Remember: those persons who have difficulty accepting themselves will also have difficulty accepting you and your strengths.

Exercise 5.6

Sit in a circle with three or four classmates and present one accomplishment you are especially pleased about, explaining the strengths you possess which helped in attaining the particular accomplishment. Allow for questions and comments. Group members may want to present additional evidence (strengths) for your accomplishment. Every person in the group should have an opportunity to tell about at least one accomplishment. If time permits, continue for a second round of accomplishments, a third, etc.

Did the group help you to discover additional strengths? List them and star (*) them in your Inventory of Strengths (Exercise 5.1). Describe in detail your reactions to this exercise. (Use additional pages if necessary.)

If you listen carefully, you will hear persons who are self-accepting praising themselves, and will seem quite natural and appropriate. You'll accept them and probably agree with their self-praise because they feel good about, and show their confidence in, themselves. So try it. At first, it may seem a bit awkward, but with continued practice, your self-praise will come naturally, and you'll find yourself accepting yourself and feeling good about yourself more often.

Exercise 5.7

Now that you've had an opportunity to praise yourself in front of classmates and receive their feedback, try praising yourself in front of three different people who do not know about this assignment. Again, remember that your praise should be honest and realistic. Try out your self-praises and write down both the praise you gave yourself and each person's reaction.

First Self-Praise:

Reaction:

Second Self-Praise:

Reaction:

Third Self-Praise:

Reaction:

This has been an exercise in our self-concept enhancement program. For self-praising behavior to become part of our natural self, part of our experiential world, we need to practice self-praises daily: at least once a day for a few days, then twice a day, etc. Again, remember that self-praise only enhances the self when we know our appraisal is honest and accurate. We have to believe our own praises before they become part of our self-systems.

Guideline 5: Praise Others

Guideline 5 deals with praising others. Although the focus here appears to be strictly on the other person, Guideline 5 also helps to enhance our own self-concept. Recall again our discussion on self-acceptance (Lesson 4). Persons who are self-accepting accept others. The reverse is also true: those persons who accept others generally accept themselves. Therefore, once we have incorporated praise for others' accomplishments into our self-systems, we'll find it easier to praise ourselves for our own accomplishments. In addition, our positive evaluations of others' successful completion of tasks and/or goals will encourage them to praise themselves; also, enhancing their self-concept should encourage their praising of us.

Mutual praising may sound phoney at first, but consider how often we congratulate a friend when he or she does something well. How often do we silently think: how nice she looks today, or he seems so happy, or I really appreciated my professor's comments on my paper. Do we tell them? Do we communicate our feelings to those persons who made us smile and feel good? Do we ever tell our friends how much we enjoyed their company? We say they already know they look nice, or we enjoyed their company, or we appreciated the understanding comment. *Do* they really know?

The following story, told by John Powell, S.J., explains vividly our need to communicate our appreciation—our praises— for others.

It was the day my father died. It was a bleak, cold, and blustery day in January. In the small hospital room, I was supporting him in my arms, when his eyes suddenly widened with a look of awe I had never seen before. I was certain that the angel of death had entered the room. Then my father slumped back, and I lowered his head gently onto the pillow. I closed his eyes, and told my mother who was seated by the bedside praying:

"It's all over, Mom. Dad is dead."

She startled me. I will never know why these were her first words to me after his death. My mother said:

"Oh, he was so proud of you. He loved you so much."

Somehow I knew from my own reaction that these words were saying something very important to me. They were like a sudden shaft of light, like a startling thought I had never before absorbed. Yet there was a definite edge of pain, as though I were going to know my father better in death than I had ever known him in life.

Later, while the doctor was verifying death, I was leaning against the wall in the far corner of the room, crying softly. A nurse came over to me and put a comforting arm around me. I couldn't talk through my tears. I wanted to tell her:

"I'm not crying because my father is dead. I'm crying because my father never told me that he was proud of me. He never told me that he loved me. Of course, I was expected to know these things. I was expected to know the great part I played in his life and the great part I occupied in his heart, but he never told me."*

The other person may not know what we're thinking and feeling unless we tell him or her. We need to disclose our thoughts and feelings to others, and what could be more enhancing to both persons' self concepts than verbal reinforcements for tasks done well or for goals successfully reached?

Guideline 5 does not suggest distorting information and falsely praising others for inferior performances. We should not be fooled by others' praises which we know to be false, and false praises do nothing for enhancing self-concept. Verbal praises for others should mirror the verbal reinforcements we give ourselves—they should be honest, accurate, and realistic, fostering, in turn, similar behavior in others.

Exercise 5.8

Verbally praise at least three other persons for their accomplishments, their successful completion of a task or goal, or their qualities or characteristics which you admire. (Just like your self-praises, your other-praises should be honest and realistic.) Include their reactions to your honest appraisals.

First Other-Praise:

Reaction:

*From *The Secret of Staying in Love* by John Powell. © Copyright Argus Communications, 1974. Reprinted by permission of Argus Communication, Niles, Ill.

Second Other-Praise:

Reaction:

Third Other-Praise:

Reaction:

Guideline 6: Help Others to Praise Themselves

Appropriately following Guideline 5, Praise Others, is Guideline 6, Help Others to Praise Themselves. By supplementing our praising others with encouraging others to praise themselves, we can help others to learn to better accept and understand themselves; this should in turn promote their acceptance and understanding of us and their praising us; and so the cycle goes.

We all know persons who degrade themselves for a characteristic or quality they possess or because they feel they lack certain attributes or abilities. It's not easy to help others to perceive themselves accurately; however, we can help others evaluate themselves more realistically, to accept themselves and to praise themselves. To accomplish this goal, we can begin by implementing Guideline 5: praising a person for positive attributes and abilities. Then we can discuss self-concept enhancement with the person, explaining all we've learned. He or she may even want to begin his or her own self-concept enhancement program.

CONCLUSION

As we pointed out in the beginning of this lesson, communication with others is crucial to our total development as unique human beings, with self-concept as an inseparable link in our communication interactions. To conclude the book we offer the following suggestions* for enhancing intrapersonal and interpersonal communication. These suggestions should be incorporated into our communication with others to facilitate the growth and development of both ourselves and those with whom we interact.

1. We communicate what and who we are, not just what we say. We communicate our own self-concept far more often than we communicate information (subject matter).

2. Anything we do or say can significantly change an individual's attitude about himself or herself—in a positive or negative way. Further, we must understand the implications for our role as persons who are important or significant to others if we are to use that role properly.

3. Individuals behave according to what seems to be true. This means that many times communication occurs, not according to facts, but according to how the facts are perceived.

4. We must be willing to deal with what a message means to different people. Essentially, we must be as willing to deal with the interpretation of a subject as we are to deal with the information about it.

5. We are not likely to get results simply by telling someone he or she is worthy. Our appraisals need to be honest and accurate. We imply the other's worth, however, through trust and the establishment of an atmosphere of mutual respect. One good way to start is to take time to listen to what others have to say and to use their ideas when possible.

6. Behavior which is distant, cold, and rejecting is far less likely to enhance self-concept than behavior which is warm, accepting, and discriminating.

7. We must be willing to be flexible in our communication with others.

Exercise 5.9

Your final exercise is to reexamine your original responses to Exercise 1.6 (Inventory of Self-Perceptions as a Communicator). Complete Answer Sheet B of Exercise 1.6 and then compare your responses with Answer Sheet A. Have you changed? How? Are you more satisfied with your self-perceptions now? Explain.

---

*From *Encounters with the Self* by Don E. Hamachek, pp. 208-209. Copyright © 1971 by Holt, Rinehart and Winston, Inc. Adapted by permission of Holt, Rinehart and Winston.

SUMMARY

Lesson 5 described six guidelines for implementing a self-concept enhancement program—a necessary component for our growth and development as communicating individuals. Since self-concept can be modified to a certain degree, we concentrated on enhancing our self-concept, which implies accepting an objective, accurate evaluation of our different selves. Six guidelines for enhancing self-concept were provided: evaluate yourself realistically, set realistic goals, concentrate on improvement, not perfection, praise yourself, praise others, and help others to praise themselves.

SUGGESTIONS FOR FURTHER READING

Coopersmith, Stanley. *The Antecedents of Self-Esteem* (San Francisco: W.H. Freeman, 1967).

LaBenne, Wallace D., and Greene, Bert I. *Educational Implications of Self-Concept Theory* (Pacific Palisades, CA. Goodyear Publishing Co., 1969).

Stewart, John, and D'Angelo, Gary. *Together: Communicating Interpersonally* (Reading, Mass.: Addison-Wesley, 1975).

PROGRAMMED REVIEW

The following pages contain a programmed review of the material covered
in this book. Work through the review in order—do not skip around. The
answers are listed to the left of the questions. Cover the answers with a tab
and lower the tab after you answer each question. If you give an incorrect
answer, go back and review the appropriate lesson before proceeding with
the review.

Lesson 1

1. Before we can begin to understand the complexities of communication with others, it is
necessary to understand _____ _____

how we
communicate with
ourselves

_____ _____ .

2. Intrapersonal communication identifies the
importance of _____ _____
in the communication process.

the individual

3. In our communication with ourselves, we process incoming information in the form of
_____ by selecting, _____ ,
and evaluating it in terms of our _____-
_____ and our _____
_____ .

stimuli, decoding
self-
concept, experiential
world

4. The core of the intrapersonal communication
process is _____ - _____ .

self-concept

5. As the model of the intrapersonal process indicates, the self-concept affects and is affected by
the _____ _____ ,
which in turn affects the entire intrapersonal
process.

experiential world

6. The stage that converts the message into meaningful symbols, dictating how the message will be
sent, is the _____ stage.

encoding

7. If the message remains within the self-system,
the encoding stage progresses to the selective perception stage as _____ _____ .

internal feedback

8 Self-concept can be defined as the individual's
total _____ _____
of himself or herself.

perceptual appraisal

physical, social
intellectual

selves

9. Our self-concept core includes all those perceptions and evaluations we have about ourselves,
including _____ , _____ ,
and _____ perceptions.

10. There are many different _____ or
dimensions that help to make up the total self.

11. There are four reasons we should be concerned
with learning more about ourselves. First, to
grow, develop, and mature into unique, pro-

communicate

ductive persons, we need to _____
with others.

12. Second, the way we interact with others is di-

self-concept

rectly influenced by our _____ - _____ .

our communication

13. Third, our perceptions of ourselves develop primarily through _____ _____
with others. As we learn more about ourselves
by obtaining feedback from others, we also

more about
others

learn _____ _____
_____ .

modify, change

14. Fourth, by learning more about how we perceive ourselves right now, we can determine
ways to _____ negative or unrealistic attitudes about ourselves.

Lesson 2

labels

15. Our self-concept develops in several ways. One
way we determine our perceptions of ourselves
is through comparing ourselves with society's
_____ .

others
social
comparison

16. A second way our self-concept develops is
through comparing ourselves with _____ ,
which Leon Festinger calls _____
_____ .

interpersonal
communication

17. Self-concept develops in _____
_____ with others.

reflected appraisals

18. We perceive who we are through the
_____ _____
of others, using those persons as mirrors to reflect our behavior.

118   Intrapersonal Communication

significant
credibility
personalism

19. The persons who have the most influence on our concept of ourselves are _____ persons, recognized by their characteristics of _____ and _____.

self-fulfilling
prophecy

20. In maintaining the person we perceive ourselves to be, we fulfill others' expectations of us, otherwise known as the _____ - _____ _____ .

selective
perception

21. We tend to see and hear information which helps to confirm our self-image and eliminate conflicting information through _____ _____ .

ignore it
accept only part
of it, accept
all of it and change
our self-perception

22. If we receive information which conflicts with our perceptions of ourselves, we usually react in one of three ways: (1) _____ _____ ; (2) _____ _____ _____ _____ _____ ; and (3) _____ _____ _____ _____ _____ _____ _____ - _____ .

Lesson 3

ourselves
others

23. To communicate effectively, we need to understand both _____ and _____ .

perceive ourselves

24. To understand and communicate more effectively with ourselves, we need to determine how other people perceive us. One way of discovering others' perceptions of us is to determine how we _____ _____ .

past experience
expectations; the way
the person actually
is; the way the
person perceives
himself or herself

25. Others' perceptions of us (and our perceptions of others) are based on a combination of the following: (1) _____ _____ ; (2) _____ ; (3) _____ _____ _____ _____ _____ _____ ; and (4) _____ _____ _____ _____ _____ _____ _____ _____ _____ .

26. To learn more about the other person, we need to discover how the other person perceives himself or herself. We can accomplish this through _____ _____ and through _____ _____ _____ _____ _____ _____ _____ _____ _____ _____ _____ _____ .

actual observation
listening to
what the other
person has to say
about himself or
herself

27. When getting to know the other person, we should consider such dimensions as the person's (1) _____ , (2) _____ , (3) _____ , (4) _____ , (5) _____ , and (6) _____ , the person's relationship with _____ and _____ _____ , as well as the person's public and private self.

ideas, attitudes
beliefs, body
voice, movement
others
himself or
herself

28. Two additional dimensions which influence others' perceptions of us (and our perceptions of others) are _____ and _____ .

roles
defense mechanisms

29. Those specified patterns of behavior which are appropriate for specific occasions are known as _____ .

roles

30. Three primary sources which determine our role-taking behavior include (1) _____ _____ , (2) _____ _____ , and (3) _____ _____ .

the other
person, the
environment, our
motives

31. Besides preferring certain roles, we also _____ with certain roles, all of which help us maintain a consistent image.

identify

32. One of the chief ways we can defend our self-concept is by using _____ _____ —five of which are (1) _____ , (2) _____ , (3) _____ , (4) _____ , and (5) _____ _____ . (Others include repression, internalization, displacement, emotional insulation, reaction formation, and regression.)

defense mechanisms
projection
rationalization
fantasy, compensation
denial of reality

33. Our personal development as unique individuals and, therefore, the growth and development of our self core, depends to a very great extent on

communication with
others

our _____ _____

_____ .

Lesson 4

the feelings
we have for ourselves

34. We need other people. Basic to the feelings we have for others are _____ _____

_____ _____ _____ _____ .

how we
accept others

35. Likewise, our feelings of self-esteem or self-acceptance determine _____ _____

_____ _____ .

reflected appraisals
selective perception
we assume others
are like ourselves

36. There are several reasons for the direct relationship between self-acceptance and other acceptance: (1) _____ _____ ,
(2) _____ _____ ,
and (3) _____ _____ _____

_____ _____ _____ .

become
socially sensitive
to one another
incorporate active
listening into our
communication
incorporate honest
communication into
our interactions

37. To accept ourselves and others, we need to understand ourselves and others. To improve self-other understanding, we should keep in mind three suggestions: (1) _____

_____ _____

_____ _____ _____ ,

(2) _____ _____

_____ _____ _____

_____ , and (3)

_____ _____

_____ _____

_____ _____ .

listen
actively

38. To view the world from the other person's perspective, we need to _____

_____ ; it requires us to respond to the other person's feelings as well as his or her words to fully understand the intended message.

paraphrase

39. To check our understanding of the message, we can _____ it, saying in our own words how we've interpreted the other person's feelings and ideas.

self-disclosure

40. Honest communication can be facilitated through sharing our feelings as well as through _____ - _____ , in which we share some personal information with another person.

situation
relationship

41. Self-growth disclosures occur primarily when the sharing is appropriate to both the _____ and the _____ .

trust
risking

42. Self-disclosures should be made in a setting of goodwill and _____ , because they do involve _____ part of ourselves.

Johari
Window

43. For each person we communicate with, we possess a different _____ _____ , which indicates our patterns of disclosure.

hidden

44. The area which contains ripe information for potential disclosures is the _____ area.

open
hidden

45. To further our development and growth as individuals, and thus enhance our intrapersonal and interpersonal communication, our task is to widen our _____ areas and tighten our _____ areas through self-disclosure.

Lesson 5

objectively, accurately
strengths
weaknesses

46. A person who possesses an enhanced self-concept perceives himself or herself both _____ and _____ , accepting both his or her _____ and _____ .

evaluate
yourself realistically
set realistic
goals, concentrate
on improvement, not
perfection, praise
yourself, praise
others, help
others to praise
themselves

47. To obtain an enhanced self-concept, we should follow six guidelines. (1) _____ _____ _____ , (2) _____ - _____ _____ , (3) _____ _____ _____ , _____ _____ , (4) _____ _____ , (5) _____ _____ , and (6) _____ _____ _____ _____ .

realistically

48.   When implementing a self-concept enhancement
      program, we should strive to evaluate ourselves
      _____ .

clearly defined
flexible
meaningful
challenging

49.   Similarly, our realistic goals should be (1)
      _____ _____ ,
      (2) _____ ,
      (3) _____ ,
      and (4) _____ .

improvement
perfection

50.   In addition, in both our evaluations of ourselves
      and setting goals, we should concentrate specif-
      ically on _____ , not
      _____ .

praise yourself

51.   Perhaps the most important guideline is
      _____ _____ ,
      because the more self-accepting a person is, the
      more accepting he or she is of others.

objective
realistic

52.   Our self-praise as well as our other praises need
      to be _____ and
      _____ .

praising ourselves
praising others
helping others
to praise themselves

53.   By _____ _____ ,
      _____ _____ ,
      and _____ _____
      _____ _____ _____ ,
      both we and others incorporate praising behavior
      and accepting behavior into our self-systems,
      thus enhancing our self-concepts.

effectively

54.   With an enhanced self-concept, we will more
      fully know, understand, and accept ourselves,
      and thus, be able to more _____
      communicate with both ourselves and others.

NOTES

1.   Ronald L. Applbaum, et al., *Fundamental Concepts in Human Communication* (San Francisco: Canfield Press, 1973), p. 13.

2.   Kenneth J. Gergen, *The Concept of Self* (New York: Holt, Rinehart and Winston, 1971).

3.   Boyd R. McCandless, *Children: Behavior and Development*, 2nd ed. (New York: Holt, Rinehart and Winston, 1967).

4.   McCandless, p. 258.

5. Donald W. Felker, "Self-Concept Enhancement: A Proposal for an In-Service Training Program for Teachers, 1971-1972 School Year," mimeographed (Lafayette, Indiana: Purdue University, 1971), p. 3.

6. Adapted from J. William Pfeiffer and John E. Jones, *A Handbook of Structured Experiences for Human Relations Training, Volume I* (Iowa City: University Associates Press, 1969), p. 19.

7. John Stewart and Gary D'Angelo, *Together: Communicating Interpersonally* (Reading, Massachusetts: Addison-Wesley, 1975), p. 23.

8. See Carl R. Rogers, "Some Observations on the Organization of Personality," *The American Psychologist* 2 (1947): 358-368; Arthur W. Combs and Donald Snygg, *Individual Behavior: A Perceptual Approach to Behavior*, rev. ed. (New York: Harper and Row, 1959); Don E. Hamachek, *Encounters with the Self* (New York: Holt, Rinehart and Winston, 1971); and Gergen, 1971.

9. See Camilla Anderson, "The Self-Image: A Theory of the Dynamics of Behavior," *Mental Hygiene* 36 (1952): 227-244; and Arthur T. Jersild, "Social and Individual Origins of the Self," *Child Pscyhology*, 5th ed. (Englewood Cliffs, New Jersey: Prentice-Hall, 1960).

10. See Hamachek, 1971; Rogers, 1947; Carl R. Rogers and Rosalind F. Dymond, eds., *Psychotherapy and Personality Change* (Chicago: University of Chicago Press, 1954); Donald W. Felker, "Final Report: Self-Concept Enhancement Program," mimeographed (Lafayette, Indiana: Purdue University, 1972); and J.W. Staines, "The Self-Picture as a Factor in the Classroom," *British Journal of Educational Psychology* 28 (1958): 97-111.

11. William D. Brooks and Philip Emmert, *Interpersonal Communication* (Dubuque, Iowa: Wm. C. Brown, 1976), p. 41.

12. Brooks and Emmert, p. 41.

13. Kenneth J. Gergen, *The Concept of Self* (New York: Holt, Rinehart and Winston, 1971), pp. 40-41.

14. Leon Festinger, "A Theory of Social Comparison Processess," *Human Relations* 7 (1954): 117-40.

15. Charles H. Cooley, *Human Nature and the Social Order* (New York: Schocken Books, 1964; c 1902), p. 184.

16. See George Herbert Mead, *Mind, Self, and Society* (Chicago: University of Chicago Press, 1934); Richard Videbeck, "Self-Conception and the Reaction of Others," *Sociometry* 23 (1960): 351-362.

17. George Herbert Mead, *On Social Psychology: Selected Readings*, ed. Anselm Strauss (Chicago: University of Chicago Press, 1964), p. 179.

18. See Arthur W. Combs, "New Horizons in the Field of Research: The Self-Concept," *Educational Leadership* 15 (1958): 315-317; Hugh V. Perkins, "Teachers' and Peers' Perceptions of Children's Self Concepts," *Child Development* 29 (1958): 203-220; Wilbur B. Brookover, "A Social Psychological Conception of Classroom Learning," *School and Society* 87 (1959): 84-87; Helen H. Davidson and Gerhard Lang, "Children's Perception of Their Teachers' Feelings

Toward Them Related to Self-Perception, School Achievement, and Behavior," *Journal of Experimental Education* 29 (1960): 107-108.

19. Wilbur B. Brookover, Shailor Thomas, and Ann Paterson, "Self-Concept of Ability and School Achievement," *Sociology of Education* 37 (1964): 271-278.

20. Davidson and Lang, p. 116.

21. Videbeck.

22. Gergen, p. 43.

23. Gergen, p. 44.

24. Gergen, pp. 45-46.

25. Gergen, pp. 47-48.

26. Leon Festinger, *A Theory of Cognitive Dissonance* (New York: Harper and Row, 1957).

27. John W. Keltner, *Interpersonal Speech Communication* (Belmont, California: Wadsworth, 1970), pp. 50-51.

28. Keltner, p. 52.

29. Adapted from Keltner, pp. 47-51.

30. Kenneth J. Gergen, *The Concept of Self* (New York: Holt, Rinehart and Winston, 1971), pp. 82-86.

31. Gergen, p. 59.

32. Don E. Hamachek, *Encounters with the Self* (New York: Holt, Rinehart and Winston, 1971), p. 17.

33. Hamachek, p. 18.

34. Defense mechanisms adapted from Hamachek, pp. 18-29.

35. Hamachek, p. 20.

36. Bobby R. Patton and Kim Giffin, *Interpersonal Communication: Basic Text and Readings* (New York: Harper and Row, 1974), p. 88.

37. Patton and Giffin, pp. 94-95.

38. Kenneth J. Gergen, *The Concept of Self* (New York: Holt, Rinehart and Winston, 1971), p. 65.

39. See Gergen, p. 66; Hamachek, p. 232; Richard M. Brandt, "The Accuracy of Self-Estimates: A Measure of Self-Concept Reality," *Genetic Psychology Monographs* 58 (1958): 89; Vaughn J. Crandall and Ursula Bellugi, "Some Relationships of Interpersonal and Intrapersonal Conceptualizations to Personal-Social Adjustment," *Journal of Personality and Social Psychology* 23 (1954): 224-252; Dorothy Stock, "An Investigation into the Interrelations between Self-Concept and Feelings Directed toward Other Persons and Groups," *Journal of Consulting Psychology* 13 (1949): 176-180; Carl R. Rogers, *Client-Centered Therapy: Its Current Practice, Implications and Theory*, (Boston: Houghton Mifflin, 1951); Boyd R. McCandless, *Children: Behavior and Development*, 2nd ed. (New York: Holt, Rinehart and Winston, 1967).

40. Hamachek, p. 231.

41. Kinch, pp. 482-483.

42. William D. Brooks, *Speech Communication* (Dubuque, Iowa: Wm. C. Brown, 1971), p. 70.

43. Hamachek, p. 227.

44. Hamachek, p. 229.

45. John Stewart and Gary D'Angelo, *Together: Communicating Interpersonally* (Reading, Massachusetts: Addison-Wesley, 1975), p. 192.

46. Allan Katcher, "Self-Fulfilling Prophecies and Active Listening," in John Stewart, ed., *Bridges Not Walls: A Book about Interpersonal Communication* (Reading, Massachusetts: Addison-Wesley, 1973), p. 85.

47. Hamachek, p. 228.

48. Samuel A. Culbert, *The Interpersonal Process of Self-Disclosure: It Takes Two to See One* (New York: Renaissance Editions, 1968), p. 2.

49. Stewart and D'Angelo, p. 171.

50. John W. Keltner, *Interpersonal Speech Communication* (Belmont, California: Wadsworth, 1970), p. 55.

51. Stewart and D'Angelo, pp. 148-149.

52. Brooks, p. 73.

53. Stewart and D'Angelo, p. 168.

54. Designed by John W. Baird, presented in Carolyn M. Del Polito and John W. Baird's "Self-Concept Enhancement in the Communication Classroom," a short course presented at the Speech Communication Association Conference, Chicago, Illinois, December 27-30, 1974.

55. Adapted from John W. Baird's exercises in Del Polito and Baird.

56. See Don E. Hamachek, *Encounters with the Self* (New York: Holt, Rinehart and Winston, 1971), p. 226; Carl R. Rogers, "Some Observations on the Organization of Personality," *The American Psychologist* 2 (1947): 358-368; Carl R. Rogers and Rosalind F. Dymond, Eds., *Psychotherapy and Personality Change* (Chicago: University of Chicago Press, 1954); Donald W. Felker, "Final Report: Self-Concept Enhancement Program," mimeographed (Lafayette, Indiana: Purdue University, 1972); J. W. Staines, "The Self-Picture as a Factor in the Classroom," *British Journal of Educational Psychology* 28 (1958): 97-111.

57. Hamachek, p. 226.

58. See Carolyn M. Del Polito, "The Development, Implementation, and Evaluation of a Self-Concept Enhancement Program," Ph.D. dissertation, Purdue University, 1973.

59. Stanley Coopersmith, *The Antecedents of Self-Esteem* (San Francisco: W. H. Freeman and Co., 1967), p. 245.

60. Wallace D. LaBenne and Bert I. Greene, *Educational Implications of Self-Concept Theory* (Pacific Palisades, California: Goodyear, 1969), pp. 28-30.

61. See Coopersmith, 1967, p. 245; P. S. Sears, "Levels of Aspiration in Academically Successful and Unsuccessful School Children," *Journal of Abnormal and Social Psychology* 35 (1940): 498-536; J. W. Grimes and W. Allinsmith, "Compulsivity, Anxiety, and School Achievement," *Merrill-Palmer Quarterly* 7 (1961): 247-271; Gertrude A. Boyd, *Teaching Communication Skills in the Elementary School* (New York: Van Nostrand Reinhold, 1970), p. 12.

62. Coopersmith, p. 238; Grimes and Allinsmith.

63. Coopersmith.

64. Hamachek, p. 243; LaBenne and Greene; and Coopersmith.

65. Hamachek, p. 251.

66. Felker and Bahlke.

Index

adjustive behavior, 67
   see also defense mechanism
antisocial behavior, 30-31
anxiety, sharing of, 82
Applbaum, Ronald L., 2
approval, 36
   and role-taking, 63
attitudes, and self-concept, 8

blind area, 83
Brookover, Wilbur, 36
Brooks, William D., 17, 77

cognitive consistency, 43
communication, model of, 76
   nonverbal, 33, 41, 77
   and perception, 4, 43, 52-54
   process, 2-3
   self-inventory, 19-26
   and self perception, 16-17, 54
comparison and self-concept, 55
compensation, 65
confirmations, 42
conflict and self-evaluation, 42
consistency in role-taking, 63
Cooley, Charles H., 34
Coopersmith, Stanley, 97
core, 7-8, 33, 72
   see also self-concept
credibility, of significant others, 40-44

D'Angelo, Gary, 16, 78, 85
Davidson, Helen H., 36
decoding, 3-4
defense mechanism, 64-67
denial of reality, 66
disapproval, 36
displacement, 66

Emmert, Phillip, 17
emotional insulation, 67
emotions, expression of, 80
encoding, 3-5, 37
environment, 43
   and role-taking, 62
      see also situational climate
evaluation, of message, 3-4, 78-80
   of self, 8
experiential world, 3

fantasy, 65
Festinger, Leon, 32, 43
feedback, 36, 43
   internal and external, 3, 5
feelings, shared, 80
free area, 83

Gergen, Kenneth J., 8
get acquainted campaign, 55-60
Giffin, Kim, 72
goals, setting of, 102-103
Greene, Bert I., 97

Hamachek, Don E., 64, 67, 74, 80, 96,
   114
hidden area, 83-84
honest communication, 80-81

I rule, 85
ideal self, 74
identification, and role-taking, 63
imaginitive thinking, 65
improvement, inventory of needs, 100-
   101
   vs. perfectionism, 103
information processing, 2
Ingram, Harrington, 83

integration, of stimuli, 3-4
intellectual perceptions, 13
    self-inventory of, 13-14, 97
internalization, 66
interpersonal relationships, 33
    see also others, significant others
interpretation, 78-80
intrapersonal communication, and communication with others, 2
    model of, 2-3
    process of, 4-5
        see also self-concept

Johari Window, 83-85
Jourard, Sidney, 91-92

Katcher, Allan, 79
Keltner, John, 53-54, 81
Kinch, John W., 37-38, 52, 74

La Benne, Wallace D., 97
labeling, 30-31
Lang, Gerhard, 36
language of self-disclosure, 85
listening effectively, 77-80
"looking-glass self," 34
Luft, Joseph, 83

McCandless, Boyd R., 8
Mead, George H., 36
medium, 4-5
message, formation, 3-4, 37
    interpretation, 79
moral-ethical attitudes inventory, 14
motives, and role-taking, 62

nonverbal communication, 33, 41, 77

observation, and self-concept, 55
others
    acceptance of, 76-77
    perceptions of, 74-77
    praise of, 111-114
    our roles toward, 62

paraphrasing, 78, 85
parents, 36-37
Paterson, Ann, 36

Patton, Bobby R., 72
peers, 36-37
perceptions
    and communication, 16
    others' of us, 52-53
    ours of others, 53-54
    selectivity of, 4, 43, 75
    of self, 54
perfectionism, 103
personal characteristics, self-evaluation of, 98
personalism, 41
physical perceptions, 8
    inventory of, 9-10, 97
Powell, John, 111-112
praise
    of others, 111-112
    of ourselves, 108-109
problem solving, and fantasy, 65
projection, 65
punishments, 36

reaction formation, 67
realism
    in goal setting, 102-103
    in self-evaluation, 97-98
reflected appraisal, 34, 75
regression, 67
reinforcement, 36
    see also rewards
repression, 66
rewards, 36
    and role-taking, 63
risk-taking, 67
roles, 8
    and expression of emotion, 80
    taking of, 60-64

"scapegoating," 66
selective perception, 4, 43, 75
self, development of, 30-49
    knowledge of, 16-17
    roles and, 60-64
self-acceptance, 72, 74-77
self-concept
    and communication, 16-17
    components of, 7-8, 11, 13
    enhancement of, 96-114

and information processing, 4
  maintaining, of, 43-44, 65
  model of, 3
self-concept core, 7-8, 11, 13, 33, 72
self-disclosure, 81-85
  exercise in, 85-90
  topics for, 91-92
self-esteem, maintaining, 65
  see also defense mechanism,
    self-acceptance
self-evaluation, realism in, 97-98
  see also self-inventory
self-fulfilling prophecy, 36-38
self-inventory
  intellectual, 13-14
  moral-ethical, 14
  outer physical, 10
  physical, 9
  social, 11-12, 97
  of strengths, 98-99
self-praise, 108-109
  helping others in, 113
siblings, 36

significant others, 36-38
  criteria for, 40-44
situational climate, 3, 4
  see also environment
social behaviors, 30-31
social comparison, 32
social perception, inventory, 11-12
social sensitivity, 77
social self-evaluation, 11-12, 97
Stewart, John, 16, 78, 85
stimuli, 3-4
strengths, inventory of, 98-99

teachers, 36-38
Thomas, Shailor, 36

understanding response, 85
unknown area, 84

values, internalization of, 66
Videbeck, Richard, 36

who rule, 85

Notes

Notes

Notes

Notes